The Reel Story

A MEMOIR

JIM CLUGSTON

Dedication

To my grandchildren,

James Andres, Jack Clugston, and Elle Clugston

CONTENTS

INTRODUCTION

I usually visit the barber shop every four or five weeks. At my age I also frequent various doctors' offices where I catch up on my reading of one- and two-year-old hunting and fishing magazines. However, I never miss reading the area fishing report that appears every Friday in the local newspaper to learn what the nearby waters have produced for some of the fishermen. Of course, poor fishing trips are seldom reported in the newspapers or magazines. Most fishing stories are bragging or perhaps an embellishment of a fair fishing trip. But some magazine stories, and I will provide proof, are simply not true. I am reminded of the wording which at one time was over the entrance door of a prominent outdoor equipment chain: "Welcome Hunters, Fishermen, and Other Liars."

While I have included many fishing stories, they are only part of my larger story. These anecdotes, my interest in fish, and the environment, and my profession as a fishery biologist help explain the direction and changes my wife Marilyn and I took during our sixty-plus years together. I describe a little about the research projects I worked on and highlight some interesting and helpful people I've encountered along the way. I've included a few travel stories and other activities to point out that aside from touching a lot of fish, I have had a diverse and, hopefully, a useful life.

Readers might recognize, as I do, that I have had a fortunate, fun-filled life in my eighty-eight-plus years, and a great deal of it was on or near water. Like every other fisherman, I have experienced poor, good, and great fishing trips. The great ones live on mostly in memory because it's only been in the last years that cellphone cameras have been ubiquitous. Although I often had a camera on board, it was usually stored in a waterproof container safely somewhere in the boat—and if the fish were really biting, it was too much trouble to get the camera out! Most photographs were taken at home after the trip.

As most people my age recognize, their expiration date is unsure but getting close. People my age may spend a lot of time thinking of the past and the experiences we had when we were young and healthy. However, looking back as I do here, I have no reason to complain. I've been lucky to have a life that has been in many ways one continuous fishing trip—complete with exciting days of great catches and beautiful scenery as well as days of disappointment when nothing would bite or the storms rolled in too early. Hopefully, my grandchildren James, Jack, and Elle—and you—will enjoy this trip with me.

Chapter 1

FAMILY

Before I journey too far, I need to recognize our parents, who made our trip possible. My mother, Evelyn Sula Daniels, was born in Gratz, Pennsylvania, on May 1, 1911. Her mother died during the flu epidemic of 1918 when my mother was only eight years old. Her father died earlier during the epidemic.

The five children—my mother, her three sisters, and a brother—were separated at their mother's death and raised by relatives. My mother was raised by her Aunt Meta (sometimes spelled Meda) and Uncle Frank Geist in Girardville, Pennsylvania. She attended Kutztown State College and earned a degree in education after two years—all that was required to teach at that time! She taught school for a few years in a one-room school at Taylorsville, Pennsylvania. A 1930 school photograph shows her with a class of twenty-three students ranging in age from grade school to a few who look as old as she (she was nineteen at the time of the photo).

My mother married James Bryson Clugston, Jr., on August 4, 1932, and was a homemaker for many years. With the start of World War II, she returned to teaching third grade in Stroudsburg, Pennsylvania, until she retired. My mother, like others in her family, suffered from polycystic kidney disease and died from complications on December 22, 1969. She was only fifty-eight. Her sisters also died of this disease in their fifties. Her brother, Paul, died in a bobsledding accident when he was twenty-one.

James Bryson Clugston, Jr., Evelyn Sula Daniels Clugston, and James
Paul Clugston (c. 1936).

My father, James Bryson Clugston, Jr., was born April 5, 1908, in Bartonsville, Pennsylvania. He was one of five boys and two girls. All were raised on their father's eighty-six-acre farm. The farm is now the site of the Monroe County Career and Technical Institute.

My father was a lineman and line foreman with the Pennsylvania Power & Light Company his whole life. He retired with a gold watch and set of suitcases after working forty-five years. He died at eighty-eight years old on May 21, 1996. His death was caused by a stroke followed by congestive heart failure.

Marilyn's parents, Gertrude and Raymond Welsh, did not join the "trip" until Marilyn and I married in 1959. They too provided much support to Marilyn and me, especially during the early years of our marriage. Ray Welsh and Gertrude Furman were both born in tiny towns in southwestern Pennsylvania. Gert's family moved to Waynesburg so the six children might attend Waynesburg College. Ray had a basketball scholarship to Waynesburg College and was the first in his family (seven children) to attend college. Gert and Ray met in college and graduated in 1928. Both began teaching high school. It was the Depression; both of their fathers had lost their jobs, so they needed to help support their families with younger siblings. Because married women were not permitted to teach in those days, they were engaged for five years before marrying in 1934.

Ray taught and coached in high schools in Uniontown, Pennsylvania; Sayre, Pennsylvania; and Bridgeton, New Jersey. Later he coached basketball at Waynesburg College and East Stroudsburg State Teachers College. When not teaching in the summers, he began scouting for the Brooklyn Dodgers baseball organization and later full time for the Pittsburgh Pirates. For several seasons, into his seventies, he was part of the Cincinnati

Leslie and Jay with Pete Rose at spring training in Tampa, Florida (March 1973).

Reds organization, going to spring training as their base-running coach. We could write a separate book about Ray's experiences.

We were fortunate to attend spring training in Tampa in 1973. After practice, our son, Jay, got his turn to run the bases like Johnny Bench, Pete Rose, Joe Morgan, and the rest of the Big Red Machine. Our daughter, Leslie, enjoyed a breakfast visit with Sparky Anderson.

Gert returned to teaching after Marilyn and her brother, Jim, entered school. She taught mathematics at Stroudsburg High School until she retired.

My Clugston uncles should be remembered for their role in World War II. Uncle Harry served as a searchlight operator in the Pacific front against the Japanese. Larry (also called Bill by the family) was a combat infantryman who was at the second landing at Normandy Beach. Only into his eighties would he tell me some stories of his time during the war; one was about his brother, my uncle Dick. Dick was stationed in Germany in an engineering company, operating a bulldozer and building bridges as the US Army advanced. Having been under constant enemy fire, Dick left the army with what was then called shell-shock, known today as PTSD. He had a tough time the rest of his life—he couldn't hold a job, he drank, and he went through a number of short-lived relationships and never married. My father tried to train him to climb electrical poles (so they could work together at Pennsylvania Power & Light Company), but Dick didn't last long doing that.

My father and Uncle Howard were deferred from the draft because they had jobs essential to the war effort. My interactions with my uncle Howard were few, but I remember one occasion when I was in junior high school. Howard needed to butcher a hog at his mother-in-law's farm. Because help was scarce with so many men serving in the war, he called me. I agreed, and I learned the process from start to finish. We shot the hog between the eyes, hung it up, and dressed (disemboweled) it. We had a large (about three feet in diameter) iron pot over a fire, and we scalded the hog in the boiling water, scraped the hair off the skin, then butchered it, creating bacon and other cuts for family use. I found the entire process interesting and learned a lot; it prepared me for later deer hunting. As a child, I even considered a career as a butcher.

During that time, the Sunday newspaper included a color map showing locations of the US troops though the information would have been several weeks old by the time of publication. I have a distinct memory of looking at the maps on Sundays

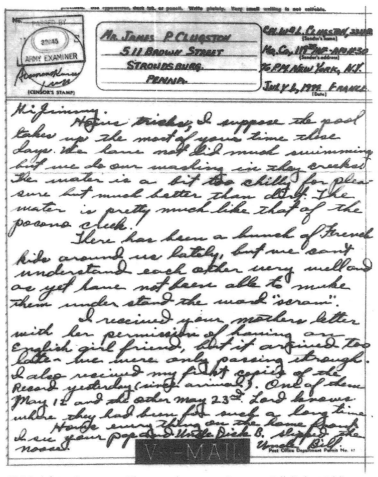

V-Mail from Lawrence Clugston, known as Larry or Bill (July 1944).

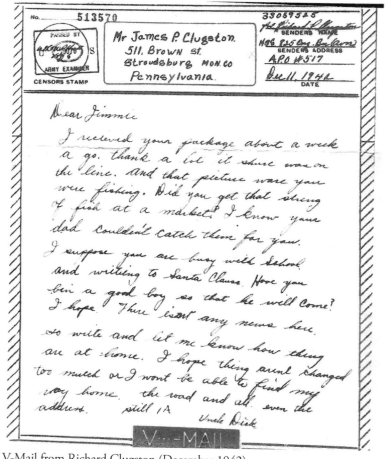

No. 513570

PASSED BY
ARMY EXAMINER
CENSORS STAMP

Mr James P. Clugston.
511. Brown st.
Stroudsburg Mon. Co
Pennsylvania.

33059525
SENDERS NAME
SENDERS ADDRESS
A.P.O. #517
Dec 11, 1942
DATE

Dear Jimmie

I received your package about a week
a go. thank a lot it shure was on
the line. And that picture ware you
were fishing. Did you get that string
of fish at a market? I know your
dad couldn't catch them for you.
I suppose you are busy with school
and writing to Santa Clause. Have you
bin a good boy so that he will come?
I hope. There isn't any news here.
so write and let me know how thing
are at home. I hope thing arent changed
too much or I wont be able to find my
way home. the road and all even the
address. still 1A
Uncle Dick

V-MAIL

V-Mail from Richard Clugston (December 1942).

when I visited my grandfather's house in Bartonsville. Our other means of learning about the troops was from Victory Mail, or V-Mail. I was always anxious to receive news from my uncles this way. The Army took letters handwritten by soldiers, mimeographed and shrunk the image of the letter to about five inches tall, and mailed that image to the family.

Chapter 2

EARLY LIFE

I grew up in Stroudsburg, Pennsylvania, which had a population of about 5,000 then. Stroudsburg was called the "Gateway to the Pocono Mountains" and wasn't far from the Delaware River. The region boasted 160 lakes, 170 miles of rivers, and the largest number of high-quality trout streams in Pennsylvania. The Brodhead Creek and Pocono Creek are well known—and they were both walking distances from my family home.

I began fishing at about six years of age when my parents rented a cabin during summers on an island in the Delaware River (see the cover picture with smallmouth bass). The upstream portion of the island was part of a golf course now called the Shawnee Inn and Golf Resort. When on the island I spent much time catching crappie, rock bass, pumpkinseed sunfish, and smallmouth bass from the bank where our rowboat was tied. Many evenings my father would take me bass fishing in the boat. Our bait was usually night crawlers or hellgrammites. Hellgrammites, aquatic larvae of the Dobson fly, were common in many of the smaller streams in the area; we would capture them beforehand and store them in a can of wet burlap until needed. Small eels were another favorite bait. My father and I would dig for them in some of the sandy areas where the Brodhead Creek joins the Delaware River.

My father and his brother Harry would take me bullhead and eel fishing in a deep hole in the Brodhead Creek, usually after dark when the eels and catfish were most active. Eels are active and slimy, and Dad and Harry taught me to grasp the eels with a small piece of newspaper to hold them as they were taken off the hook. Cleaning the eels and bullheads was my father's job. Eels are excellent eating—I do remember my mother's chagrin as they appeared to squirm in the frying pan when their muscles contracted as they fried.

On my grandfather's farm, about six miles from Stroudsburg at Bartonsville, there was a small spring-fed stream about four feet wide and a foot deep. I spent much of my time at the farm catching minnows and crayfish by hand and building small dams, which was great fun for me. The stream supported native brook trout, often about six inches long. I learned early on that I could catch these fish with small worms. Uncle Dick taught me how to sneak up on a pool to watch the trout scatter and then come to rest under a rock or other cover. Then using a fine wire (like a piano wire) snare, we would slip the noose over the trout's head and *jerk!* Though it was good sport, it couldn't have been a legal way to catch trout. I trust the statute of limitations has long expired.

I know in these early grade-school years, I truly became "hooked" on fishing. During grade school and junior high, I was always eager to fish whenever my father or an uncle would take me. Also, in those years, young people weren't constantly supervised as they are now. Towns were far more walkable than they are today, and young people had freedom go off to explore on their own. Consequently, friends and I often walked to small ponds not far from my home to fish for bullheads and sunfish. We would go to a pond behind the firehouse or to a series of other ponds known as "the Brickyard" because they were formed by excavation for the making of bricks. These ponds were also popular for ice skating during the winter.

I rode my bicycle to reach fishing spots a little farther from home. I remember biking to a deep pool in the McMichaels Creek near Glen Brook Country Club. McMichaels Creek was a little warmer than the other nearby streams and not the best place to catch trout. I remember catching a three-pound smallmouth

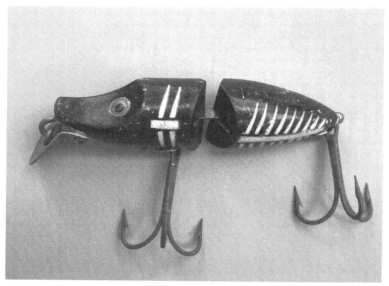

Heddon River Runt (1945).

bass there on a black and white Heddon River runt. I still have this lure, and it's part of my wall-mounted collection.

During junior high school, a friend's mother planned a one-day trip for us, on our own, to New York City. A passenger train left East Stroudsburg early mornings and went directly to the city. Our itinerary showed an exact schedule of where we would use other transportation to end up where we planned to go. The highlight for me was to visit a big fishing store, perhaps a

Herters. I purchased a number of Devon Minnow spinning lures
that were made in England. The lure had four very sharp treble
hooks. At that time, I think Pennsylvania limited lures to three
sets of hooks, so one set of hooks was cut off to make them legal.
Despite their origin, they were great trout lures in the Poconos—
and no other fishermen appeared to have them.

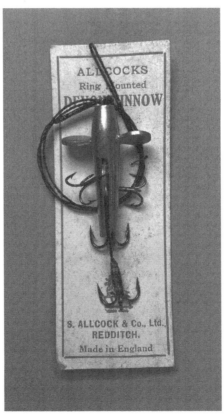

Allcocks Devon Minnow spinning lure.

Chapter 3

EDUCATION AND MILITARY SERVICE

During high school, I continued to fish in the Delaware River, local streams, and ponds as much as school activities and social life would permit (girls!). Studying did not consume much of my time. About 1948, my father purchased a twelve-foot Penn Yan Cartop boat that weighed 125 pounds. He equipped it with a 5.4 horsepower Evinrude motor that had four cylinders. We frequently fished a mile section of the Delaware River, near Bushkill, Pennsylvania, that was usually isolated by rapids both upstream and downstream of the section. Except for an occasional canoeist, we usually had that section of river to ourselves. We carried the boat and motor about one hundred yards from the River Road to reach the river. We usually used nightcrawlers, madtoms, and hellgrammites for live bait and some of the more common fishing lures at that time made by Creek Chub Bait Company, Heddon, Shakespeare, Albagas, and a lure called "flatfish" made by Worden. We caught smallmouth bass, various other members of the sunfish family, pickerel, and walleyes. The walleyes were often caught by trolling with a nightcrawler attached to an "Indian Joe Spinner."

I used one of Shakespeare's first fiberglass spinning rods and an open-faced Airex spinning reel. I also used a True Temper metal casting rod with a Pflueger Skilkast fishing reel. My father

Penn Yan Cartop boat (1948).

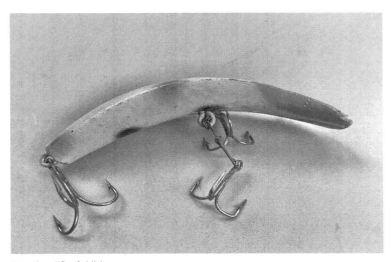

Worden "flatfish" lure.

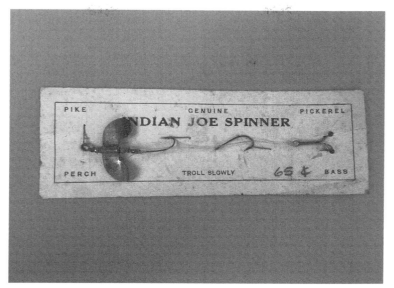

Indian Joe Spinner, three hooks.

used a Bristol steel rod and a Shakespeare Criterion reel. Braided line was on all reels—monofilament line did not become available for fishing until about 1959. The two casting rods still hang on my office wall. Not many people used the slow-moving flatfish lure, but it was one of my favorites. It came in many colors and sizes, and rainbow trout couldn't resist this lure when they wouldn't strike conventional spinners.

At that time, April 15 was usually the start of trout fishing season in Pennsylvania. Because it was usually still quite cold then, there would be ice on the banks of the creeks and the fishing line often would freeze in our rod guides. The opening day always was an excused absence from school (as was the first day of deer season).

Prior to trout season, the State stocked trout in public trout streams. The Pocono Mountain Sportsmen Association usually assisted the stocking by carrying milk cans full of trout upstream and downstream from the stocking truck—probably to come back on opening day to fish the specific areas where they placed fish. I recall that my chemistry teacher endorsed a day off from school to help with stocking—as long as I told him where we put the fish. I doubt it helped my grades. Somehow, during the stocking a large trout or two slipped into my hip boots and made it to the frying pan at home for dinner. I know this was not the intent of the State's stocking program.

While I was in high school, my father purchased a 1950 Oldsmobile 88. It was unique at that time because the front windshield was a single piece of glass. The car was nice, but more important to me was that I then inherited his 1936 Pontiac. The Pontiac provided me the opportunity to explore fishing waters a little further from home. Plus, the girls in high school appeared to like a young man with a car.

During high school one of my favorite hangouts was MacNichol's Sport Shop. Mac was always busy tying trout flies and smoking his pipe. He taught me much about fishing and occasionally took me trout fishing at his private fishing club. Some readers might remember when yellow signs were posted on front doors of homes if someone inside had measles, chicken pox, mumps, or some other contagious disease. Mac gave away yellow signs that said "Warning Fishing Pox—Very Contagious to Adult Males." I've had the sign from Mac's store since I was in high school, and I've put it up in my garage everywhere I've lived.

Summers during junior high school and high school I had various jobs to keep me in spending money. I worked in a dry-cleaning plant, as an electrician's helper, in a Sears and Roebuck warehouse (and later as a salesman), and as a "grunt" in the construction of my uncle Larry's new home. Despite these

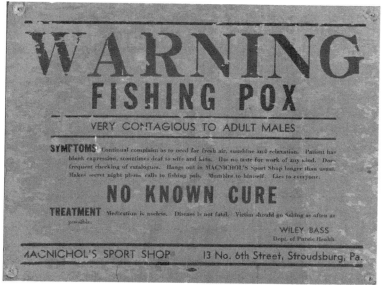

Fishing Pox sign from MacNichol's Sport Shop, Stroudsburg, Pennsylvania.

summer jobs, I always found time to fish in the evenings or on weekends with my father, but many times by myself.

I graduated from high school in 1951 and ventured to Penn State to study electrical engineering—what a mistake! Engineering was the major profession for male students to seek, and there appeared to be no college to consider other than Penn State. Following two years of fraternity life (Kappa Delta Rho) and not very good grades, in 1953 I was drafted to help end the Korean War, which did end about a month after I was sworn in. I did get one "A" at Penn State—in a course on "techniques of trout fishing and fly tying" offered by George Harvey, then considered the dean of American fly fishing. I know he took presidents Dwight D. Eisenhower and Jimmy Carter fishing in Spring Creek and other streams not far from campus. Harvey lived to be ninety-six. Fishing must be good for your health.

Before I was drafted in the Army in 1953 and during a summer break from Penn State, Bill, a fraternity brother and I spent about two weeks fishing in the Thousand Islands of the St. Johns River between New York State and Canada. His grandmother owned one of the small islands between Gananoque, Canada, and Clayton, New York. It was a small cottage on about an acre of sparsely vegetated rock. The family had an elegant Gar Wood mahogany runabout for transportation from Clayton to the island. I do not know the boat's length, but I remember two small cockpits and an inboard engine. We were not allowed to use the Gar Wood boat while on the island, but we could use a fourteen-foot metal boat with an outboard motor. We fished continuously around the islands for smallmouth bass and northern pike and trolled for muskellunge (or muskies) in the open waters. We caught one undersized muskie. Northern pike were really big fish to me (compared to the fish I caught in Pennsylvania), and to prove how big the pike were, I took one whole, frozen fish home with me on a commercial bus. I guess a photograph was not enough proof. On one Sunday while on the island, everyone dressed up, and we took the Gar Wood to Gananoque to go to church. I remember entering the harbor with tour boats all around and the passengers appeared to be gawking at this privileged family—if they only knew!

US ARMY

I spent most of my Army time, April 1953 to May 1955, at Fort Belvoir, Virginia, and Fort Hood, Texas. Fort Belvoir was only about thirty minutes away from Washington, DC. I spent much of my free time at the various museums, parks, and other public places I could afford on my private first class (PFC) salary. On a three-day pass I sometimes visited my parents in Pennsylvania.

While in Texas on weekends or on a three-day pass (which I could also earn for donating blood), I explored and fished the nearby reservoirs—unlike what my barrack buddies did in their free time.

On one trip to Inks Lake (really a reservoir) in my 1947 Studebaker Starlight Coupe, both banks of the tailrace were lined with fishermen using bait on cane poles to catch white bass as they concentrated at the base of the dam. Using a small trout spinner with my old Shakespeare rod and Airex Spinning Reel, I caught fish nearly every cast. It's the truth! Other fisherman appeared amazed at the rapidity with which my strange fishing gear caught fish. And they were Texans! I did move between fishermen and gave them the fish I caught.

What did I really do while in the army? Following basic training at Fort Leonard Wood, Missouri, I was transferred to Fort Belvoir, Virginia, to take a course in engineering drafting. After completing the course, I remained at Fort Belvoir to teach blueprint reading to heavy equipment operators. This was not very exciting, and I expressed my desire to go overseas—I did not care in which direction. I was told if I put in for a transfer, there was no guarantee where I would go. I gambled, put in for a transfer, and ended up in Fort Hood, Texas. There my excitement continued by designing garbage can racks and other structures around the camp, plus some typing. Fortunately, I had enough time remaining and took a course in electric motor and generator repair back at Fort Belvoir. Following that course, I returned to Fort Hood, where I served my remaining time as a typist—almost full-time! A camp-wide inventory was ongoing twenty-four hours a day, and this process required typists. I volunteered for the night shift and worked about four nights a week with three nights off. This schedule gave me a long weekend every week, so I had a great opportunity to visit my parents in Pennsylvania or to visit nearby lakes. I normally slept until about noon after working at night, followed by a visit to the camp swimming pool to work on my tan. And now you also know why I never rose above the rank of PFC.

Chapter 4

A CIVILIAN AGAIN

I served my military requirements and was discharged in April 1955. In early summer of that year, I teamed up with Don Garaventi, a high school friend, and we drove to Canada in his mother's 1947 Ford Ranch Wagon with my Penn Yan boat on the roof. I do not remember our route or if we had a specific destination. As we entered Canada, we saw a large billboard that read, "Highway Route in Vicinity of Charleston Lake." However, the area had many smaller lakes, and I think we just picked one at random. The lake was undeveloped except for a farmhouse, and there we received permission to camp and fish. We pitched our tent on a small peninsula that provided good shoreline fishing. We caught many smallmouth bass, pickerel, and I think, yellow perch. I am not sure how many days we fished, and I do not remember fishing any other lakes on that trip.

In August 1955, hurricanes Connie and Diane brought destructive flooding to much of eastern Pennsylvania. Nearly seventy people died in the Stroudsburg area, and many homes were washed away. My father had parked his car near an electric power station in the lower part of Stroudsburg, and it was totally submerged. He fortunately was elsewhere and not harmed. Our home was in the highest part of town and not damaged. However, the surrounding streams were littered with all kinds of debris. Consequently, the once-beautiful trout streams were bulldozed and straightened the following summer to reduce

Don Garaventi, entering Canada (1955).

future flood damage. It wasn't a fun job, but I spent that summer
with a work crew that included a bulldozer and about ten men
with axes. We worked to clear the streams and made large piles
of debris for burning. It was a strenuous, hot, and smoky job.
While the pay was especially good for that era, my favorite trout
streams became unfishable. I had no desire to fish elsewhere that
summer.

COLLEGE: SECOND TRY

Following the summer of hurricanes, floods, and hard work, I
returned to Penn State with the benefits of the GI Bill. I majored
in zoology with the possibility of becoming a veterinarian. However, as I finished my bachelor of science degree in zoology, I was
offered an assistantship in the Fish and Wildlife Department of
the University, so I began my master of science degree in fisheries
biology.

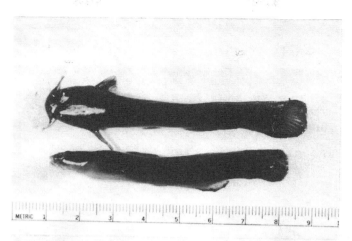

FIGURE I. THE COMMON EASTERN MADTOM, *Noturus insignis,* COLLECTED IN THE BALD EAGLE CREEK, CENTRE COUNTY, PENNSYLVANIA.

For my master's thesis, I worked on the life history of common eastern madtom in Bald Eagle Creek, not far from Penn State. The madtom, locally called a stonecat, is a member of the catfish family. At first glance, you would think it is a young bullhead. However, it rarely reaches six inches long. Madtoms have an adnate adipose fin, which means the fleshy adipose fin is continuous with the caudal fin or tail. Also differing from most freshwater catfish, they do have a toxic gland at the base of the dorsal and pectoral spines and can deliver a painful sting. They generally are nocturnal, and very few people know of their existence. Fishermen, however, know they are excellent bass bait. The best way at that time to collect madtoms for bait was to strike a flat rock in the stream very hard with a metal pipe. The shock would stun the fish, and they would float downstream where we could catch them with a small net. For my study, we used what now would be considered a very primitive electrofishing system. We pulled a specially-made small boat that contained a basic 250-volt generator. A fellow student and I waded upstream, prodding under rocks or ledges with hand-held electrodes and dip nets at the end of long wooden or fiberglass rods. We always wore very heavy-duty rubber gloves to avoid electric shock.

Today electrofishing is a major collecting tool of fishery biologists. They are commercially made to use from boats and on backpacks, and the electric output is adjustable to work in waters of different quality. Collected fish are usually weighed, measured, sampled for other needed information, and returned to the water unharmed from their "shocking" experience.

While working on my master's degree, I also worked as a laboratory assistant for a zoology professor. One of my jobs was

FIGURE 2. COLLECTING MADTOMS IN THE BALD EAGLE CREEK. A 230 VOLT D.C. ELECTRIC SHOCKER IS TRANSPORTED IN THE BOAT.

to conduct "live" experiments that were viewed through a micro-scope and shown on a screen when the professor lectured in a large seminar room. One of his lectures required me to show live human sperm through the microscope—the sperm he provided. Later, while walking through campus I was asked (with a grin) a number of times, "Where did the sperm came from?" Another of his lectures required the showing of human blood through the microscope and onto the big screen. In front of the camera, he collected the blood from *me* using an old spring-loaded lancet rather than the simple handheld lancet that most are familiar with. He wanted to be sure he got enough blood—and he did! Again, as I walked through campus, students I didn't know would ask me "How's your finger?" I suddenly became a Big Man on Campus! The following school year this zoology course became a television course, and I continued to do laboratory work in front of the television camera. At that time, photograph-ing ahead of time was not considered, so if an experiment didn't work, or if I goofed up, the television audience in State College and surrounding areas, including Pittsburgh, saw it!

This professor was also on my graduate committee. I learned food was a major interest in his life. In preparation for oral exams in defense of my thesis, I correctly predicted one of his questions: He asked if madtoms were good to eat. I had fried a few big ones beforehand (remember six inches is about maximum size), and I was able to say "yes—and they taste like catfish." My thesis did result in my first peer-reviewed scientific publication.

Chapter 5

A WEDDING AND A FIRST JOB

I graduated from Penn State with a master of science degree in fisheries biology on June 6, 1959. Near the end of my studies at Penn State, I had begun to search for employment. George, a fellow fishery student, and I drove to Michigan in the middle of winter to interview for jobs with the state agency. Later we were both offered jobs in trout research. However, jobs were not available for about six months. George accepted and I declined. I had other plans, such as marrying Marilyn on June 13, about a week after graduating, and I needed some income. I was also offered a job studying salmon on Kodiak Island, Alaska. However, because of limited housing at the research facility, the position required a single man sharing housing with a married couple. I declined that offer too.

I found a job of interest advertised by the Florida Game and Freshwater Fish Commission. I had never been close to Florida in my life. Fortunately, that year the Annual Meeting of the American Fisheries Society was held in New York City. My major adviser at Penn State, Dr. Ed Cooper; another student; and I attended that meeting. The chief of Florida's Fisheries Division, Ed Heinen, also attended, and I arranged to interview for the job open in Florida.

The interview went well, and I was offered a job at a location uncertain at that time (we later learned I was to report to Tallahassee and then continue to Leesburg for my assignment). The official offer came in a letter dated April 7, 1959. I'm including my offer letter—one an unemployed graduate student could not turn down even if he had never been to Florida or knew where he would be living.

After our wedding on June 13, 1959, Marilyn and I visited Cape Cod on a week-long honeymoon. I was advised not to take any fishing gear on our honeymoon (and there was lots of water where we were going!). Marilyn and I returned to Stroudsburg for a week and packed our limited belongings (mostly wedding gifts) into my 1957 Plymouth station wagon prior to our journey to Tallahassee. We arrived June 30, a day before my reporting date of July 1. The summer heat was staggering—especially to Yankees—and we settled into a hotel with a swimming pool. Frolicking in the pool, Marilyn splashed me, and, in an attempt to dodge the water, I turned my head suddenly, breaking my nose on the pool ladder. Much of the rest of the evening was spent in the Tallahassee Memorial Hospital emergency room. I reported to work the next morning to meet the staff and complete paperwork despite being unable to speak easily and with my broken nose fully taped. Reporting to work with a broken nose two weeks after getting married was the subject of many jokes at staff meetings and get-togethers for years afterward.

My first assignment was at the Leesburg research office where I became acquainted with more paperwork and protocols of being a State employee. A number of biologists and aides were stationed there, and I accompanied them on various research sampling ventures. I experienced sampling techniques I never learned in graduate school. Pulling in a seine with a six-foot

Game and Fresh Water Fish Commission

TALLAHASSEE

April 7, 1959

A. D. (BOB) ALDRICH
DIRECTOR

Mr. James P. Clugston
206 W. Beaver Avenue
State College, Pennsylvania

Dear Mr. Clugston:

I had intended writing you since returning from New York, but have been out of the office almost constantly and didn't get to it. Today, I had just started a letter to you, when yours arrived.

I am glad that you will be able to join us and I believe it would be best to report here July 1st. We can fill out the necessary employment papers then and then head on down to Leesburg in the central part of the state. You will probably be assigned there temporarily, and then maybe to our Vero Beach office. That can be decided once we have a chance to get together.

Our starting salary at the moment is $380 per month with a good chance of an increase to $400 by July 1st. I can guarantee the former figure, but only hope for the $400. At any rate, raises and promotions are according to our Merit System standard, based on one's own initiative and ability to assume additional responsibilities. All equipment, including vehicles, will be furnished by the Commission. There will be a certain amount of traveling involved for which we have a $9.00 per day expense account for lodging and meals. Out of state per diem is $12.00.

Other benefits include group insurance policies, two weeks annual leave, 14 days paid sick leave, and of course, cheaper living because of low fuel and clothing expenses. You will also find pleasant working conditions and an exceptional group of fine co-workers. I am confident you will enjoy working with our staff and equally confident that they will be glad to welcome you to the fold.

READ *Florida Wildlife* —FLORIDA'S OWN OUTDOOR MAGAZINE

Mr. James P. Clugston   -2-   April 7, 1959

Awaiting your arrival in Tallahassee, I remain,

                                Very truly yours,

                                GAME & FRESH WATER FISH COMMISSION

                                E. T. Heinen

                                E. T. Heinen, Chief
                                Fishery Division

ETH:br

alligator in it was really something different for one fresh out
of Penn State! Although work generally started at 8 a.m., I also
learned that there was no rush to get to work. Work often began
at a local diner for more coffee or another establishment for a
beer or two. I drank some coffee but no beer at that time of day.
One biologist stationed at Leesburg worked with homeowners who lived around the many small lakes of Central
Florida. His job was to keep track of water quality, help solve
vegetation problems, and evaluate the fish populations. On one
occasion our visit included water skiing with the owner's boat.
Despite the relaxed attitude, we worked hard and accomplished
a lot. There was camaraderie among biologists throughout the
State. When help was needed, other biologists and aides showed
up. If any of us visited another area to help and we had to stay
overnight, we regularly stayed at the host biologist's house and
the $9.00 per diem went toward refreshments.

Helping other biologists was also an opportunity to become
acquainted with other parts of Florida. On some occasions,
Marilyn was able to accompany me. One trip, which she still
talks about, was to Lake Trafford, a 1500-acre lake near the town
of Immokalee. The town was very rural with one movie theater
open one night a week and temporary homes for migrant field
workers. Harold Moody, the biologist I was helping, arranged
for us to stay in a "fish camp" on the lake. The cabin was as
rustic as you can find. The outhouse was a ten-yard walk over
a boardwalk surrounded by water and swarms of mosquitoes.
The mosquitoes also occupied the outhouse—which mandated
a rapid return to the cabin. Harold cooked us dinner and cleaned
the pots with readily available Spanish moss. After retiring for
the night, Marilyn turned on a light and discovered the cabin

walls covered with large wolf spiders—and that was the end of her night's sleep!

Harold, who graduated from a small college in Pennsylvania, was one of the first biologists to work in Florida. He was eccentric and a bit of a naturalist. He collected artifacts and other specimens during his travels and taught me a lot about Florida. Following our sampling on Lake Trafford, he took Marilyn and me back into a cypress swamp to see the wild orchids that grew on the cypress trees. It was a new and beautiful sight for these Yankees.

Settling in Leesburg, Marilyn and I rented a two-bedroom apartment over a garage in a rather upscale residential area on the shore of Lake Harris. I could easily walk to nearby shorelines to fish in the evenings. Marilyn and I also enjoyed exploring and bass fishing in Lakes Harris, Griffin, Yale, and connecting streams and canals. Early on, employees were allowed to use work boats for personal recreation, and the same was true for our assigned vehicle. The basic rule was never to park the state vehicle in front of a bar—*behind* it was okay. A few years later the state ruled that State cars could not be taken home or used for other personal needs.

After a busy six months in Leesburg, I was assigned to Fort Lauderdale to study the fish populations in a portion of the Everglades known as Conservation Area 2, and we stayed there for four years. It was 137,000 acres of mostly saw grass enclosed by dikes and canals. The area was created to retain water during hurricanes and rainy seasons and to hold irrigation water supplies in time of drought. The area had an interior levee, which created Pool 2B, locally called the "bombing range"—a popular bass fishing spot. This area was about one-fifth of Conservation Area 2. The State cut trails in Pool 2B for fishermen. Airboats were necessary to travel north of the interior levee. I think I was the first fishery biologist to work full time in the area. Since I was a Yankee fresh out of Pennsylvania, I was fortunate that two wildlife biologists doing deer research in the area showed me the territory and the art and skill of getting around in an airboat. What a job!

Sport fishing was great in the canals and saw grass areas. The exterior canal on the eastern border contained small tarpon (five to ten pounds) and an occasional snook. Gene Surber, a well-known visiting scientist who developed some of the best quantitative samplers for benthic invertebrates (still on the market today), wished to catch a tarpon on a fly rod. I took him to the canal and found many rolling tarpon. He had a number of strikes, hooked and lost a few, and finally landed one about five pounds. He went home to Virginia very happy! Gene died on June 3, 2021, at the age of seventy-nine.

Gene Surber (c. 1960).

Largemouth bass were readily caught along the edge of the interior canals and throughout the saw grass areas. Four- and five-pound bass could easily be caught with a Johnson weedless spoon. A major problem for the bass fishermen was that bowfin (or mudfish as commonly called in the South) and Florida spotted gar were everywhere. Both species would strike your lure and are good fighters but not generally desired to put on your table to eat. The gar did lots of striking, but their small, fine teeth and long, bony mouths made them difficult to hook. If you really wanted to land a gar, the technique was to attach a small piece of felt to a spinner, and their fine teeth would get caught in the felt.

The major objective of my research in the Everglades was to estimate the abundance and diversity of the fishes in the saw grass areas. Little was known except what was reported by sport fishermen. Basic fish collecting for identification was usually done by electrofishing from an airboat. To estimate the population abundance, we employed a block-net that was five feet deep and, if deployed in a square, would enclose one acre of water. Rotenone, of the proper concentration, was applied to the enclosed area, and all dead fish were collected for two to three days, identified, weighed, and measured. At this time, I had two fishery aides working with me. Killing the fish attracted brown water snakes, water moccasins, alligators, and birds, who all took advantage of a free lunch. We estimated between fifty to one hundred fifty pounds of fish per surface area of water. The amount of fish and species present depended upon the kind and amount of aquatic vegetation and the water depth. We collected at least twenty-five species of fish from the saw grass area. We handled lots of dying, dead, and partially decomposed fish in three days under the Florida sun. It was a smelly job!

Mudfish sampled in 1962 Everglades survey. (Mike Gaddis, "Bass Dilemma," *Florida Wildlife* [October 1965]: 22–26.)

Periodically pool 2B would dry up and result in massive fish kills. Such an event occurred in the early winter of 1961–1962. The area steadily shrank until remaining fish were isolated in small pools scattered throughout the area. In an effort to save fish, local sportsmen groups worked with dip nets and garbage cans to transport bass to six waiting tank trucks donated

Hand-captured largemouth bass from Everglades Conservation Area 2B as it was drying up (1962).

by local tackle shops to move fish to Pool 2A. Simultaneously, a crew and I worked with my electrofishing airboat to collect and tag fish that were transported to Pool 2A. We collected 151 bass that weighed 650 pounds. I am unsure of the number of fish moved by the sportsmen, unfortunately. Area 2B dried up rapidly; only a few inches of water remained, and the backs of fish were sticking out of the water. Recognizing that most remaining fish would die, the Florida Game and Freshwater Fish Commission removed all limits and catch methods—the fish were "up for grabs." A Miami newspaper said, "tons of bass are being gigged, clubbed, and even grabbed by hand." It was a strange sight—like hundreds of vultures sweeping down on dead carcasses on the road.

About three months later, another drought-related event developed. Conservation Area 3 to the west of Area 2 was not diked, and the marsh had direct access to surrounding canals.

As that marsh gradually dried, fish were forced into the canals. The canals became overcrowded, and there was a heavy fish kill because of low dissolved oxygen levels. Most of the fish that died were bass and other sunfishes. Those that remained, as determined by our sampling, were mostly bowfin and Florida spotted gar.

Consequently, to help the local fish camps and their clients and to jump-start the canal fishing, we treated about seventeen total miles of three different canals with rotenone. We estimated about 40,000 pounds of fish were killed and 95 percent were bowfin and gar. Some connecting canals were not treated so that those fish would move in and help repopulate the area. The State stocked 90,000 bass fingerings in late May—fish that could reach nearly a pound and were capable of reproducing the following winter.

By this point in my career, I had already touched a lot of fish, and I also learned to leave my clothing at the door when I came home for dinner!

I was especially interested in largemouth bass growth rates and reproduction. I mentioned earlier that four- and five-pound bass were common and—unlike the lakes of Central Florida or South Georgia—"lunkers" were never caught (at least by me or by my sampling program). Water temperatures provided a near year-round growing season. However, their growth appeared to slow during the heat of the summer, which is the reverse of growth patterns in the more temperate latitudes to the north.

In 1960 I received permission to use some small drainage ponds on the Fort Lauderdale airport and some ponds on the Florida Turnpike rest areas for research. I stocked fingerling largemouth bass from Florida and fingering largemouth bass from Iowa in the ponds. They were sampled monthly to determine growth rates and degree of sexual maturity. This research led to my first paper, which I presented at a national meeting of the American Fisheries Society in Jackson Hole, Wyoming, in September 1962.

Reaching Jackson Hole for that meeting was an adventure. The assistant director of the Florida Game and Freshwater Fish Commission, the chief of the Fisheries Division, and I flew from Tallahassee to Jackson Hole in a four-seat twin-engine airplane. The pilot was a retired bush pilot from Alaska and didn't mind flying low so we could see the wildlife. We only got lost once, landed at the wrong airport to refuel, and consequently saw a lot of additional country on the way to Wyoming. After the meeting, the assistant director needed to stay an extra week, but we brought the director of the Game and Fish Commission from Tennessee with us to drop him off in Nashville. We did see a lot of the United States on that trip!

During the four years working out of Fort Lauderdale, I frequently fished the Everglades, the many canals of the "Venice of America," and the waters flowing to the Atlantic Ocean. Mac, the fishing tackle shop owner from Pennsylvania I talked about earlier, retired and moved to Hollywood, Florida—not far from Fort Lauderdale. I was able to repay him for the trout fishing trips he treated me to when I was a young man. I know he enjoyed fishing for bass with me in the conservation areas. Mac and I often drove to some of the nearest bridges in the Keys in the evening and fished for snook, tarpon, and any other species that would strike our lures. We both lost lots of lures and fishing lines. Fishing from land or from a bridge meant we couldn't chase a big fish like we might if we had been on a boat, but we had lots of good stories!

I also gained another great fishing companion while living in Fort Lauderdale. Marvin Iuen was a building contractor who would fish every evening if he had no family or work conflicts. We devoted a lot of nights to fishing for snook under Fort Lauderdale bridges. We also made "surf rods" from long Calcutta bamboo poles by tying guides and a tip to the poles with electrician's tape and attaching a Garcia Mitchell 302 saltwater spinning reel to the rod with metal hose clamps. We fished at night from the beach near some jetties using large mirrOlures. Snook fishing seemed best at night, plus we needed to walk (trespass) on some private homeowners' beaches to reach our fishing spots.

Bill Herke was my direct supervisor and stationed in the Vero Beach Office of the Florida Game and Freshwater Fish Commission. At times I assisted him with his research. On one such occasion we were told the bluefish were running in the nearby inlet.

Bill, like me, was a Yankee and relatively new to Florida, with most of his fishing experiences in freshwater. After we completed our work, we took a small outboard motorboat to the inlet. There, with mirrOlures we caught bluefish around eighteen inches long on almost every cast. Because of their sharp teeth, the plugs soon lost their identity and lost all color and shininess, but it did not seem to make any difference to the bluefish. I do not remember how many we kept but later learned we kept too many. I soon learned they taste too "fishy" and are even stronger-tasting after freezing. Much later in life I learned to "bleed" them when caught, vacuum-pack them, then grill them within a few days after capture. Those techniques improved their taste, but they still aren't my favorite fish to eat—but they are a strong fighting fish and fun to catch.

Our parents visited Marilyn and me from Pennsylvania a number of times to take advantage of the warm winters in Fort Lauderdale. My father was a fisherman, but my father-in-law was not. I often took my dad fishing in the Everglades and in the canals scattered throughout Fort Lauderdale. We also fished in the Florida Keys for spotted sea trout, various snappers, and many other species readily available.

In July 1960, my parents, Marilyn, and I joined a "party boat" and fished in the Atlantic Ocean adjacent to Fort Lauderdale. I don't remember the exact number, but probably thirty or forty people dropped baited hooks over the side. It was a poor trip, but my father caught an eighty-eight-pound black tip shark. Returning to the dock, the captain—I guess to advertise a successful fishing trip—hung the shark from the back of the boat for tourists at the marina to see.

Before we left, I asked to cut the jaws from the shark. The captain was reluctant at first and said it was illegal. I showed my Florida Game and Fish Commission identification and told him I had a collecting permit. My bluff worked, though I don't think taking the jaws was illegal. During the "operation," we quickly drew a crowd of spectators. Later I preserved the jaws in formaldehyde, and much later I cleaned all the flesh covering the layers of teeth needed to replace those that are lost because of use and age. I gave the cleaned jaws to my father to show off to fellow workers in Pennsylvania. The jaws now hang in my home office.

Between 1961 and 1964, the Florida Game and Freshwater Fish Commission conducted a statewide fish-tagging program. The program was sponsored by the Joseph Schlitz Brewing

Jaws from 88-pound black tip shark caught by my dad, James Bryson Clugston, Jr., Ft. Lauderdale, Florida (July 1960).

Company. Ten species of fish were jaw tagged with rewards from $25 to $10,000. Over 28,000 freshwater fish were tagged and released into 120 lakes, rivers, and canals throughout the state. Biologists throughout the state spent many hours collecting and tagging fish in their own areas of the state—I know I did my share of tagging in South Florida. The program provided useful fish growth and migration information. I do not remember if anyone caught a fish valued at $10,000. I do know that at the close of the contest, in my area of South Florida, 112 tagged fish were recaptured that were worth $3,775 to local anglers. I am not sure if the promotion helped sell more beer!

While the tagging program was ongoing, I received a request from the Tallahassee office to show a visiting administrator from the Schlitz home office the "Everglades." He and his attractive wife—both overdressed for airboating—came to my office in

Fort Lauderdale. We proceeded to Andytown to launch my airboat. At that time, Andytown consisted of a gas station-convenience store-restaurant and a phone booth. (Demolished in 1979 to make way for part of I-75, Andytown is no longer on any map.) I need to point out my airboat was a work boat, a little big and heavy with only a seat for the boat operator. Coworkers or guests needed to stand behind the driver—and hang on! I took a leisurely trip to an area where I knew there would be wading birds and perhaps alligators basking in the sun. Unfortunately, I drove a little too slow on a bend in the trail and I got stuck. The only way to free a stuck airboat is to get out and push. And they did, good-naturedly, in about six inches of muck. The airboat became free and we returned safely back to the boat ramp. They thanked me for the "experience." I was unsure if I would have a job the next day, but I never heard anything about it from Tallahassee.

Much of the research I and other biologists conducted throughout the state were partly supported through the Federal Aid to Fish Restoration Program. Consequently, we were periodically subjected to visits from the Atlanta and Washington, DC, Fish and Wildlife Service's offices to ensure we were following our research plans and spending federal money as intended. Most visits were useful, but some "inspections" seemed like excuses to get out of a big city, especially during the winter. Some brought their golf clubs and others a little fishing gear. I, of course, was always ready to help with their fishing gear.

I remember one visit from Washington that was to help plan a joint study between the US Fish and Wildlife Service and the National Park Service (NPS). This reconnaissance trip required airboating from the National Park Service's station on the Tamiami Trail through the Shark River Valley in the Park, a distance of about twenty or twenty-five miles. We used two airboats, one supplied by the park ranger and the other by me. The park airboat could take two guests, and I took one. And, just in case, I had some fishing gear stored under the front deck of my airboat.

We stopped along the way several times to observe and talk about water levels and aquatic vegetation. This was the true Everglades, where water was very slowly moving to the South and Florida Bay and was not impeded by levees as were the Conservation Areas to the north. We reached our destination about noon. During our lunch break, I broke out my fishing gear—enough to share.

If we cast floating mirrOlures toward the mangroves, it was easy to catch three- to four-pound bass. If bass failed to strike early, a nice snook ended up in the boat. After a little more exploring, we returned to the ranger station. I left the state not

Noon-day catch (snook), Everglades National Park (March 1961).

long after that field trip and don't know if a research project ever developed between these agencies. I also don't remember what happened to the few fish we caught; perhaps they ended up in the ranger's freezer?

I fielded many strange requests because I had access to an airboat in South Florida. A rather well-known outdoor writer wished to write an article about bass fishing in the Everglades. Our Tallahassee office asked me to help him and make sure that he caught some nice bass. As a bit of insurance, an aide and I visited the area a day prior to his visit and captured some nice bass by electrofishing and placed them in a floating live box that we used occasionally during our research. We met at Andytown early the next evening for a night fishing trip. The writer and a fishing guide were in one airboat; a photographer and I were in a second airboat. We traveled a short distance to my live boxes—and the action began! The guide and I hooked the bass we previously caught to his lure, and the photographer took shots of him landing them and holding them up in the guide's airboat. Later the photographer sent me copies of the fishing "action," which I still have. The article was published in the April 1964 issue of a popular hunting and fishing magazine with the photographs of the faked catch. The action in the article accompanying the photographs, except for the bass in the boat, did not happen that evening. The author was a gifted writer and produced an interesting article—but that was one heck of a fish story!

We left Fort Lauderdale in 1963 to move back to Leesburg when I was promoted to director of the State's fishery research laboratory. In the 1960s, Leesburg was a sleepy southern town of about 8,000 people. There were two restaurants, an A&W root beer stand where you could get a shrimp platter, one movie theater where you could go to cool off on a hot night, and a few motels. The local joke was that "the only excitement in Leesburg was when the 'B' burned out on the Big Bass Motel sign." However, my bass fishing greatly increased and improved with the availability of the large chain of lakes in the surrounding area. At that time, pitching soft plastic worms into the vegetated edges of a lake was a popular method to catch bass. Marilyn became quite efficient with this method, and we had a lot of cheap dates on lakes Harris and Griffin. I never caught any of the real "lunkers" (over ten pounds) the area was noted for, but I did catch an eight pounder on a black Johnson spoon in Little Lake Harris about two weeks prior to moving on to my next job. I had that bass mounted as my Florida souvenir, the only fish I ever gave to a taxidermist.

Chapter 6

BECOMING A FED

I worked for the Florida Game and Freshwater Fish Commission for about seven years and then became interested in a federal position. When I learned that most desirable biologist jobs went to those already working for a federal agency, I accepted a position with the Bureau of Commercial Fisheries in Galveston, Texas. At the time, it wasn't the most appealing job available. My assignment was to study shrimp population dynamics in the Gulf of Mexico. Once again, I was jumping into an unfamiliar environment where I lacked training and experience. It turned out to be a great job, and Galveston was a fun place to live.

I quickly learned about the shrimping industry by visiting the local shrimp processing plants. I also found myself out to sea, trolling for shrimp, for a few days at a time. The laboratory trawler was modified for research and did have an air-conditioned cabin. Most trawling was performed at night with days available for sleeping, swimming, and a little fishing. Occasionally, rough storms came up and I did get seasick a number of times.

Marilyn and I rented a house in Galveston across the street from Offatts Bayou, where the spotted sea trout fishing was good. The house, affordable but unfurnished and much too large for Marilyn, our Weimaraner Heidi, and me, contained a number of high-water marks from past hurricanes that Galveston is well known for.

Marilyn and I often went to the beach. I fished in the surf, Marilyn sunbathed and swam, and our dog chased shorebirds up and down the beach. Gafftop catfish were plentiful; these fish were strong fighters and good table food compared to hardhead catfish, also caught in saltwater. We ate a lot of fresh jumbo shrimp as a byproduct of my research. When we ate at restaurants, fresh scallops and oysters were always available. Galveston was a seafood lover's paradise.

While in Galveston, I decided it was time to purchase my own boat. I bought a 1966 sixteen-foot MFG Beachcomber that had a tri-glide hull. Initially it had a forty-horsepower Evinrude. A few years later I upgraded it to a seventy-horsepower Evinrude. It was an ideal fishing and family boat and served us—and much later our children—for many years. Now, my daughter, Leslie, and her family have it. It has been on water in Texas, Georgia, South Carolina, Florida, North Carolina, Kansas, and Arizona in its fifty-five years.

1966 16-foot MFG Beachcomber with Kevin, James, and Leslie Andres in Surprise, Arizona (2021).

TO THE BIG CITY

I remained in Galveston for two years and in 1966 took a position with the US Fish and Wildlife Service in Atlanta. My job was in the Division of Federal Aid with the responsibility of reviewing the status of federally supported research projects ongoing throughout the Southeastern states. Because there was a lot of travel involved, I acquired a fishing rod kit from Herters, then a popular outdoor equipment store, and made a spinning rod that came apart to fit in a small backpack or case. I used an ultralight spinning reel with four-pound test line and carried a spool of eight-pound test line just in case. During evenings and off-hours while traveling, I fished all kinds of waters in these states. I also had several pocket-sized tackle boxes filled with lures appropriate to the location I visited. I was always well prepared.

Atlanta was the largest city Marilyn and I ever lived in. However, there were two large reservoirs just about an hour away, Lake Lanier and Lake Altoona. Marilyn, our Weimaraner, and I often visited them with my outboard motorboat on weekends to swim, water ski, and fish for largemouth bass. We sometimes took a few friends to have a picnic in the evening.

Lake Lanier is on the Chattahoochee River and discharges water from the bottom of the reservoir cold enough to support trout. The State stocked rainbow trout in these waters, and, not far from Atlanta, trout fishing was available. My fishing companions and I wore chest waders and drifted sections of the river in a float tube—though we'd have to get to the nearby shore to warm up. I used ultralite spinning gear in these waters.

One spring, some co-workers and I had some good fishing trips on the Etowah River, which flows into Lake Altoona, catching white bass on their spawning run. I also remember a long weekend fishing trip to Carrabelle on the Florida Gulf coast, about three hundred miles from Atlanta. Despite living in the big city, I did manage to go fishing!

We experienced both tragedy and joy while in Atlanta. In October 1966, Marilyn's brother, James (Jim) Raymond Welsh, a Navy helicopter pilot, died during a fire on the aircraft carrier USS *Oriskany* while serving during the Vietnam War. Jim received numerous citations for heroism and extraordinary achievement in aerial flights as a helicopter pilot. He made many rescues at sea, some under threat of enemy fire, flew over 310 plane-guard missions for returning *Oriskany* strike pilots, and completed several medical evacuations. Jim made national news as a "Hero of Rescue" when he helped rescue forty-four Chinese crewmen from a floundering freighter during a typhoon in the South China Sea. Jim Welsh was twenty-seven years old when he died.

The USS *Oriskany* had seen combat operations off Korea from 1952 to 1953, and off Vietnam from 1966 to 1973. The ship was decommissioned in 1975 and was to be used as scrap. However, in 2006 the carrier was sunk twenty-four miles off Pensacola Beach to serve as the world's largest intentionally created fishing reef.

We were blessed in January 1968 to adopt our son, James Raymond (Jay). He was a great catch—a real keeper!

BACK TO SCHOOL

Over the decade of the 1960s, the US Fish and Wildlife Service began a new program at universities throughout the United States called Fish and Wildlife Cooperative Units. Unit leaders were required to have a PhD and to serve as faculty and teach at the specific university. Assistant leaders were expected to have a master's degree and good field experience to complement the leader and assist in training and research. The units were funded by the US Fish and Wildlife Service and the state wildlife agencies in the host state. The host university provided office and laboratory space plus secretarial support.

Assistant unit leaders were given the opportunity to pursue a PhD, and their research, with university approval, could be used for the dissertation. The assistant leader position is one that I coveted a few years prior, and in 1968, I did succeed in obtaining this position at the University of Georgia in Athens.

My research was focused on the effects of heated effluents on largemouth bass and bluegill sunfish at the US Atomic Energy Commission Savannah River Plant near Aiken, South Carolina. The plant was developed in the early 1950s with a number of reactors and other nuclear production facilities. A canal-cooling reservoir system was used to dissipate the hot water discharged from two of the reactors. Two of the reservoirs with varying degrees of elevated water temperatures, Par Pond and Pond C, were the sites of my research.

One of the primary objectives of my study was to determine the behavior of largemouth bass in the thermal mixing areas and cooling reservoirs. I gathered data with temperature-sensing ultrasonic transmitters surgically implanted in bass abdomens. This phase of my research was much more enjoyable than the very laborious sampling of the general fish populations. Bass tracking was done both day and night. When a specific bass was located, the water temperature was recorded, and the water temperature indicated by the bass transmitter was recorded. To determine fish location in the dark, I placed small lighted markers of different colors on foam floats around the lake because GPS technology to fix locations was not yet possible. One evening I could not locate a specific marker; a few days later, I found it on the shoreline with multiple teeth marks from a curious alligator. They were very abundant in the lake, so I never swam on the job!

Par Pond was the major cooling pond available for my research. For security reasons, neither the pond nor the plant itself was accessible to the public, so the pond supported an unexploited fish population. The water temperature of most of the lake was similar to other lakes at that latitude. However, an arm or cove of the lake received the discharge from Pond C, a much warmer cooling pond, through a large culvert. Large-mouth bass concentrated in this heated effluent. Fish numbers were large and could be caught nearly every cast with any lure. My supervisors in the Atlanta Regional Office and in Washington, DC, learned about the prolific fishing, and I soon received numerous visits by supervisors to witness (and enjoy) this fishing experience. We supplied our visitors with the best lure, called the "mermaid plug," but the truth was, it was difficult to find a lure the bass would not strike.

The move to Athens provided many more fishing opportunities. The area had many lakes and farm ponds for bass and bluegill fishing, and trout could be caught in some of the streams of North Georgia. There were also beaver ponds scattered throughout the area in many of the small streams. A co-worker, Mel Huish, introduced me to the sport of wade-fishing in the beaver ponds. Sometimes using a float tube—and always using a fly rod—we caught bass as well as bluegill, redbreast sunfish, long-eared sunfish, spotted sunfish (also known as a stump-knocker), all locally called bream. They all had beautiful colors. At that latitude we did not need to worry about water moccasins or alligators.

Beaver pond catch, near Athens, Georgia (1975).

Marilyn and I fished some private waters in Athens and made another great catch. In July 1970 we adopted Leslie Ann. She was a red-haired beauty, long for her age but within the slot limit, so we could keep her!

My responsibilities in Athens included the management of some ponds at the Fort Gordon and the Warner Robins Air Force Base. I periodically visited both to assess the fish populations. Their main needs were good fishing, so it was necessary to include the rod and reel sampling techniques on these visits. Blue catfish were stocked in some Fort Gordon ponds. They are native to the Mississippi River Basin and were introduced throughout eastern states as a management species. They grow large compared to most catfish and are fun to catch. However, as with many fish introductions, problems have developed between native populations in some areas of the country.

The School of Forest Resources at the University of Georgia maintained a large research area near campus. Some of my research was conducted in a number of plastic swimming pools on that site. There also was a small lake the Fishery Unit maintained as a bass-bluegill fishery. Our son, Jay, first learned to fish on this pond; Leslie kept busy catching tadpoles.

Chapter 7

TIGER COUNTRY

I received my PhD in 1973 and continued to serve as assistant unit leader at the University of Georgia until 1975 when I moved to become chief of the Southeast Reservoir Investigations in Clemson, South Carolina. Conversion from a Georgia Bulldog to a Clemson Tiger soon began. The Clemson laboratory was a part of the US Fish and Wildlife Service's National Reservoir Research Program. The Clemson laboratory was charged with evaluating the effects of various electric power production plants on all aspects of fish populations in the lakes on which the power plants were located. Principal reservoirs studied by the Clemson laboratory were lakes Jocassee and Keowee. Lake Jocassee was the upper reservoir in a pumped-storage system, and Lake Keowee was the downstream reservoir receiving and storing the water that passed through the Jocassee turbines during the day when electricity was most needed. In the evening, the turbines were reversed, and water was pumped back to Lake Jocassee so that the water was available for power generation the following day. Lake Keowee also served as a cooling reservoir for a Duke Power Company Nuclear Power Plant on its shores.

Both reservoirs provided good bass fishing. Because of a depth of about three hundred feet, Lake Jocassee had a "two-story fishery." The State of South Carolina stocked rainbow and brown trout to enhance the sportfishing. During the cool winter months water temperatures were satisfactory for trout survival.

However, in the summer, surface waters became too high for trout survival and the trout moved into the deep, cool water of the lake. Fishermen had to troll with downriggers to catch the trout in the deep water where many of the trout grew as large as fifteen to seventeen pounds.

Due in part to the proximity of the federal laboratory to Clemson University, I became an adjunct associate professor at the university. This status, in turn, helped joint research projects between the university and the laboratory. I served on a number of university committees and occasionally provided a seminar. I also taught a course in aquaculture on my own time, with my superiors' approval, to help the university when it suddenly lost a faculty member.

The town of Clemson, along with Clemson University, is on the banks of Lake Hartwell. Lake Hartwell and the Keowee River, which flowed a short distance from Keowee Reservoir into Lake Hartwell, were excellent fishing waters. I particularly enjoyed fishing the Keowee River because it had limited access with few other boats on the water, and largemouth bass and white bass were readily available. I specifically remember one evening I took Leslie with me. She was then eleven years old and getting into fishing. I saw the vegetation moving near shore and told Leslie to cast her surface plug (probably a Rapala) near that spot. She made a perfect cast—the water exploded—and she landed a beautiful seven-pound bass. The tailrace of Keowee Reservoir, water flowing in to the Keowee River, provided excellent shoreline white bass fishing when they concentrated there in the spring.

Housing was limited when we moved to Clemson, so we rented a small house not far from the laboratory and the university. The house next door was owned by a university professor

Leslie with 7-lb. largemouth bass caught in
Keowee River, South Carolina (c. 1981).

who liked to fish as much as I did. Doyce Graham had a small
fiberglass boat and knew Lake Hartwell well. We became good
friends and fished together on evenings and weekends as often as
our jobs would permit. We took turns on whose boat we would
use, partly depending on our destinations. Later, Marilyn and
I built the house of our dreams on a hilltop with a view of the
hills to the east. After we moved, Doyce and I continued to fish
together. A boat ramp into Lake Hartwell was just a few miles
from our new house, and our family enjoyed many weekends
boating, water skiing, and sometimes picnicking on a sandy
beach.

At that time, Clemson had a population of about 7,000
people plus about 11,000 students at the university. It was a picturesque college campus at the foot of the Blue Ridge Mountains.

Its nearness to larger cities (Anderson, Greenville, and Atlanta) and the availability of sporting and cultural events at the university prompted Marilyn and me to consider the area as a place to retire. As a federal employee, I had no idea where I would be working when I reached retirement age, so we purchased a third of an acre on a secluded deep-water cove on Lake Keowee. It was about a forty-minute drive from Clemson, and Marilyn and I took the kids (and dog) there to swim on the weekends. Also, a few years after I purchased the Lake Keowee lot, the US Corps of Engineers began auctioning parcels of land around the shores of Clark Hill Reservoir. At that time, waterfront property was becoming scarce, so, thinking it might be a good investment, I bid on a two-acre parcel—and won. The lot was probably an hour and a half drive from Clemson, so as a family we rarely visited it. My visits were usually with a chainsaw to clear and improve the site.

Doyce and I fished mainly in Lake Hartwell at the edge of Clemson and in lakes Keowee and Jocassee. On one occasion we deviated from our normal fishing spots and, with a borrowed canoe, we floated and fished a section of the Savannah River downstream of Lake Hartwell Dam. In a long day, we covered about seven miles. There were many mild rapids and massive boulders in the riverbed. We fished with ultralight spinning gear and caught lots of yellow perch. Thanks to the cool water released from the bottom of Lake Hartwell, the water temperature was cool enough for yellow perch to thrive—perhaps near the most southern range of the species.

Somehow, Doyce lost his glasses in a pool about six feet deep. The water was clear, and I could see the glasses on the bottom, but we could not hook them or retrieve them no matter what we tried. But Doyce needed his glasses, and—because he couldn't see them—I undressed to my underwear and dove into the cold water. After I retrieved the glasses, I dried and we resumed our fishing trip. My Ford F-100 was parked at the spot we planned to debark (I'm unsure of how we shuttled vehicles or if someone helped us). My truck had a shell on the back and a built-in bench that served as a storage area with a nicely upholstered cushion that Marilyn had made. During our time on the river, someone broke in and stole tools as well as the cushion from the back of the truck. They did not break into the cab, so we were able to return safely home. Marilyn was upset a long time about the loss of the cushion that she had worked so hard to make.

A few years after our trip, a new dam was completed near the upper reaches of Clark Hill Reservoir. The new reservoir, Lake Russell, began filling in October 1983 and was full by December 1984. The new reservoir flooded and covered much of the stream habitat that Doyce and I canoed on—perhaps never to be seen again.

During my career there was one particularly difficult period in terms of research productivity. The time was especially stressful for my family and me and my entire staff. During 1980–1983, there was continuous pressure to close numerous federal fish hatcheries and federal research laboratories to reduce federal spending. Consequently, the National Reservoir Research Program was closed in 1983—which included the Clemson facility. The laboratory was well along with long-term fishery studies that were abruptly brought to a halt, wasting time, data, and money.

Chapter 8

GATOR COUNTRY

About the same time, two other events occurred to help direct my future. While federal fishery research laboratories and fish hatcheries were being closed throughout the country, in 1983–1984 Congress provided $5.25 million to build the National Fisheries Research Laboratory in Gainesville, Florida. Because of uncertainties regarding the status of the fish population in Everglades National Park, the Fish and Wildlife Service, in cooperation with the National Park Service, was requested to conduct appropriate research in Florida Bay. I was selected to direct the study, oversee construction of the Gainesville laboratory, and serve as scientific director of the facility in Gainesville, so, in 1983, we moved to Gainesville.

The study first involved finding and hiring a staff of twelve, establishing a field office, developing a research plan, and writing an environmental assessment, which was a part of the National Park Service's needs. Because the NPS didn't approve of some of the Fish and Wildlife Service's sampling techniques, I needed numerous endorsements to move forward with my research plan.

One endorsement is worthy of mention. With the help of Art Marshall, a friend and fellow federal employee from Vero Beach, I had the opportunity on July 22, 1983, to spend an hour with Marjory Stoneman Douglas at her cottage in Coconut Grove, Florida. Art knew her well and set up the meeting. Marjory Stoneman Douglas is best known as the author of

The Everglades: River of Grass. She kept calling me "young man"—at the time of the visit, I was fifty and she was ninety-three years old. We discussed my research plans but probably spent more time talking about the plight of the Florida panther in the Everglades. On leaving and walking out through a small pantry, she asked me to open a jar of homemade jam. I did, and suddenly hundreds of tiny ants covered my hand. Douglas was nearly blind at that time, and I explained the situation and disposed of the jar in an outside garbage can. She did not ask me to open another jar. I did leave with her approval of my plans. Marjory Stoneman Douglas, nationally known as the first lady of conservation, died at the age of 108.

The University of Florida provided twenty-five acres to accommodate the Gainesville laboratory and research ponds. Construction of the 21,000-square-foot office and laboratory began in February 1984 and was completed in October 1985. Construction of a maintenance building and twenty-one research ponds was finished in 1988. During this period, I held countless meetings with contractors, site inspectors, and the Denver Engineering Center of the Fish and Wildlife Service regarding progress, changes, and myriad unforeseen problems. Selecting and purchasing furniture and major laboratory equipment plus recruiting and hiring core laboratory staff were also my responsibility—most of which I never trained for as a fisheries biologist.

The Gainesville laboratory was charged with the maintenance and restoration of both anadromous fish populations in Southeastern rivers and coastal areas and freshwater and estuarine species that were environmentally imperiled in federally managed waters. We also were to evaluate the beneficial and harmful effects of the exotic fishes introduced into the United States and to examine the life histories and status of endangered or threatened fish species in the Southeast. With the ongoing National Park study in Florida Bay and laboratory responsibilities, I had lots of waters to explore. Fortunately, I acquired a great, enthusiastic, and productive staff to do the hard work.

After about four years of initiating research projects to meet laboratory objectives as scientific director, the Washington office of the Fish and Wildlife service upgraded the laboratory to a "center." Fishery laboratories in Marion, Alabama, and Stuttgart, Arkansas, became part of the new center's responsibilities. Consequently, a gentleman from Washington, DC, with much more bureaucratic experience than I had became the center director. I, in turn, became director of the anadromous and estuarine programs. The change came with less responsibility, more fun, and no change in salary. Not a bad deal!

With the changed responsibilities, I was able get out in the field more frequently and became directly involved in various research projects. At the Merritt Island National Wildlife Refuge, we initiated a study that required catching and tagging spotted sea trout. Using a rod and reel was the best method of catching spotted sea trout, and then we measured, weighed, and tagged them before releasing each fish unharmed. We worked on another project in Florida Bay in the Everglades National Park. That fish population study allowed me to visit the nearby Keys with a rod and reel in the evenings to fish or enjoy a Florida lobster dinner in one of the numerous restaurants in the Keys.

Closer to home, most of my research focused on studying endangered Gulf sturgeon in the Suwannee River. Our studies included sampling much of the river from the Georgia state line to the Gulf of Mexico—a distance of about two hundred miles. I boated all portions of this river except the area known as Big Shoals. I boated to the top from upstream, but I was never brave

8-pound spotted sea trout caught at Merritt Island National Wildlife
Refuge, Florida (April 25, 1992).

enough to go through these rapids in any type of watercraft. I fell in love with the beauty and diversity of the Suwannee River, and in my will are instructions for some of my ashes to be scattered into this great river.

The university community of Gainesville is an ideal location for anyone, working or retired, who enjoys outdoor activities such as boating and fishing. The university's sporting and culture events are always ongoing and a big advantage to living in the area. Numerous lakes are within an hour's drive from Gainesville. Orange Lake is currently producing record-size largemouth bass. Many small lakes and ponds are scattered throughout the area. The Suwannee River and the Ocklawaha River are two scenic environments to fish for largemouth bass and other sport fishes.

Chapter 9

SALTWATER
FISHING
IN RETIREMENT

Before moving to Gainesville, my saltwater fishing had been limited to our time in Ft. Lauderdale, the two years we lived in Galveston, and a few short fishing excursions over the years. However, Gainesville was only an hour and a half away from the Atlantic Ocean to the east and the Gulf of Mexico to the west. Similar to my luck in Clemson, about two blocks away a gentleman had a fourteen-foot jon boat in his driveway. After a few discussions, we began fishing together. Chuck Taylor, a retired engineering professor, taught me much about fishing the "skinny" water at Shired Island near Horseshoe Beach and in the small creeks near the mouth of the Waccasassa River. This of course, was in his jon boat, which was light enough for us to get out and pull it over oyster bars if needed. He stressed the importance of knowing the tide schedule when planning a fishing trip.

One fishing trip to Shired Island is hard to forget. Shired Island boat ramp, at that time, was isolated. We probably spent three to four hours fishing and returned to the ramp with a satisfactory catch of spotted sea trout. However, when we returned to the boat ramp, his boat trailer was missing—and there wasn't a soul in sight. I returned to Gainesville, leaving Chuck to guard our boat and gear, and returned with a borrowed trailer (from my lab) to get us home that night.

Chuck and I used my MFG Beachcomber in the nearshore areas of Cedar Key, at Seahorse Reef, and in the east and west passes of the Suwannee River. We caught a lot of spotted sea trout and redfish over the years we fished together. He and his wife left our neighborhood in about 2008 to live in a university retirement community. Chuck died when he was ninety-three. His obituary read in part, "Fish trembled at the mention of his name." It was true; he was a good fisherman.

With the closeness of Cedar Key and the other sites, I soon became addicted to saltwater fishing because we always caught fish (well, almost always). Consequently, my freshwater fishing became limited to pond fishing with my grandchildren in Gainesville at the pond behind Jay's house and while on a vacation in my hometown in Pennsylvania. There I usually managed to catch a few trout in the Pocono Creek, which flows behind Marilyn's parents' home. Sometimes I would fish in streams I frequented when I lived in Stroudsburg just to see how the environment changed over the years—plus catch a fish or two. On one visit I ventured to a section of the Bushkill Creek just upstream of where it flowed into the Delaware River. I parked my car near the trail I planned to take and encountered a black bear eating berries along the stream bank. I retreated slowly back toward my car and watched the bear move slowly past me, eating berries as it went. I do not remember if I caught any trout, but fishing does have a lot to offer even if you do not catch anything!

Marilyn and I also enjoyed canoeing in the Delaware River during these visits, and I was able to cast for smallmouth bass between strokes. We used a canoe rental/shuttle service to take us to Smithfield Beach where we started our ten-mile float to the small town of Portland, Pennsylvania. The trip, depending on our swimming, picnicking, and a little fishing, lasted about four hours. Most of our float was through the Delaware Water Gap National Recreation Area—an especially picturesque and restful area. We also passed through the area where my father and I often fished with his Penn Yan boat when I was in high school—more good memories.

The switch to saltwater fishing and the vastness of waters available to fish prompted me, in 2000, to buy a 19.5-foot Key West Bay Reef center console boat. It was designed for near-shore boating and fishing a little offshore with caution. Initially it was powered by a 115-horsepower Evinrude. In 2006, I upgraded to a 140-horsepower Johnson four-stroke outboard motor. The boat was perfect for taking three people fishing, six people boating and sightseeing, or visiting the springs in the Suwannee River.

I purchased a sixteen-foot Gheenoe and a six-horsepower Evinrude motor for the shallow backwaters of Cedar Key and Shired Island. These waters were especially productive for spotted sea trout, redfish, and occasionally flounder. The Gheenoe looked like a high-sided canoe with a square end for the motor. It was best to have a fishing companion who didn't mind getting off the boat and pulling it over shallow areas. As most serious fishermen know, one boat cannot get you everywhere.

I retired from the federal government in October 1995 after being employed by various agencies for about thirty-six years. At that time the federal government again was making efforts to reduce their number of employees and offered a very generous

Retirement party with Marilyn, Leslie, and Jay, and gift of stained-glass sturgeon; Austin Cary Forest Lodge, Gainesville, Florida (September 16, 1995).

early retirement package—and being very uncertain of what was next, I took the offer.

After I retired from the federal government, I continued to complete some research papers on my own time. Thanks to much help from Ken Sulak (whom I hired in 1994 and who inherited some of the messes I initiated), the information was published in appropriate journals. I also was invited to assist with the Florida Game and Freshwater Fish Commission's snook-tagging project. The event was near the State's Tequesta field laboratory not far from Jupiter Inlet. Rods and reels were the only sampling gear needed. We caught (I landed three) numerous large snook in the boat that I was in.

My fishing companions varied over the years. I usually found someone eager to go fishing and, when much younger, I would go by myself just to get on the water if no one else could go

Snook-tagging, near Jupiter Inlet, Florida.

with me. During my early salt water fishing years, in addition to Chuck Taylor, often Marilyn, Jay, some of his friends, Leslie, and some friends from work would accompany me to fish along the Gulf Coast. As children will do, they went to college, found jobs, got married, and consequently were not around to go fishing.

Marilyn, who loved to be on or near the water whenever she could, was often very busy.

While in Fort Lauderdale, Marilyn spent a year at the University of Miami to receive her Florida teaching certification. After our move back to Leesburg, she taught seventh-grade science. In Galveston, she was a research laboratory technician at the Shriner's Burn Institute. We moved to Atlanta and Athens, then to Clemson, where she was a stay-at-home mom. In Gainesville she worked as a technician at Pharmatec, a drug development company. Later, she became the director of the Clothes Closet of the Gainesville Community Ministry, which helped people in need in the area. She also was a church coordinator for Family Promise of Gainesville, a nonprofit group that assists homeless families with children. I also worked with Family Promise by serving on the fundraising committee. We held a large fund-raiser at Northwest Grille each Christmas where Santa and Mrs. Claus visited with the families and took free pictures with the children. Many families attended to see the Clauses and have dinner, and the restaurant donated a portion of their sales to Family Promise. Another event is the annual Bed Race. This year was our seventh-annual race, it always draws a crowd and local news coverage, making it a very effective fund-raiser.

FISHING AT CEDAR KEY

During my retirement I continued to fish at Cedar Key, at the mouth of the Suwannee River, Steinhatchee, and many of the shallow backwaters and tidal creeks between these sites. Redfish and spotted sea trout were my favorite targets. I spent a lot of time at Seahorse Reef, about seven miles from Cedar Key marker number 1, where seasonally Spanish mackerel were abundant. Spotted sea trout, young gag grouper, bluefish, jack crevalle, ladyfish, small sharks, cobia, and numerous other species could be caught out there. Much of the time I fished with a ¼-ounce leadhead jig with a red or white head and various colored and shaped soft plastics attached to the jig. Occasionally, if the bites were slow, I would include a section of shrimp on a jig head. Sometimes we would fish with live shrimp underneath a bobber or a popping cork, and we always caught something. I also used various plugs such as a mirrOlure or Rapala. A slow-moving, sinking mirrOlure was great during a cold winter when sea trout would congregate in the deep waters at the mouth of the Suwannee River.

I purchased my Key West boat with the idea of venturing a little farther offshore than I would go with my old sixteen-foot MFG. We made a few trips when the seas were smooth and caught some gag grouper by trolling eight- to eleven-inch deep running plugs such as Rapala and Mann's Magnum. I never developed the skill or technique of fishing with live and frozen bait near the bottom for grouper or snapper. I never became an offshore fisherman; I disliked the long boat ride to reach the right spot because it felt like wasted fishing time.

About the time I purchased my Key West boat, I learned Tom Lovegrove, a friend from church, was shopping for a fishing boat. I invited him to fish with me to help him decide what he wished to purchase. Tom soon became a very willing fishing companion and fished with me for many years—and Tom never did buy that boat! But I did gain a good friend and reliable fishing companion. Being retired, we usually stayed off the water on weekends unless we had out-of-town guests to take out. Weekends were for those who still spent forty hours a week doing their jobs and needed to get on the water! Boat ramps and trailer parking spaces also were much less crowded during weekdays.

Tom and I fished mostly out of Cedar Key with occasional visits to the mouth of the Suwannee River and to the town of Steinhatchee. We seldom fished farther offshore than Seahorse Reef and an area known as "spotty bottoms" out of the west pass of the Suwannee River.

Over the years, many others fished with me. One avid fisherman I need to mention is Grover Smart. Grover had worked in the University of Florida Department of Entomology since 1964, teaching and doing research. Grover was an active member of Trinity United Methodist church where he sang in the choir and taught Disciple Bible classes for about forty years. I only fished with Grover a few times; I wish there had been more. Grover had a serious heart problem and Parkinson's disease. During our last fishing trip with Francis Davis, he said something to the effect of "If my heart gives out, don't try to make it back to shore—you won't make it, so keep fishing. I don't want to mess up a good trip!" Grover was ninety years old when he died in 2020.

A friend from Georgia, Kim Primmer, visited a number of times. On one trip in early February 2003, he, Tom, and I did a charter offshore fishing trip out of Cedar Key. We returned with a limit catch of gag grouper. I remember well because there is a photograph of me holding a thirty-three-inch grouper in the February 2003 *Woods 'N Water* magazine. I guess this is a little bragging?

Francis Davis, another friend from church, retired from the University of Florida in 2008. Francis grew up in South Carolina and Alabama, not far from water, and fished with his father. He is an accomplished boater and fisherman and was always eager to fish when we all got the urge. From that time on, probably until 2018, Tom, Francis, and I fished together three to four times a

33-inch gag grouper from charter fishing trip, Cedar Key, Florida. It was the largest of a limit catch that included a 30- and 31-inch grouper (2003).

month—as often as we could considering the demands of family, travel, weather, and tides.

Our fishing effort was mostly at Cedar Key, Florida, where we caught many spotted sea trout near shore and Spanish mackerel and other species at Seahorse Reef. Unfortunately, in early 2018 our usual trips slowed and eventually stopped. I developed some health issues; the polycystic kidney disease that took my mother's life caught up with me. On July 17, 2019, I had surgery to place a catheter in my abdomen and shortly after began the life-saving process of peritoneal dialysis, something I do every night as I sleep. I am free to do much of what I want during the day. However, the process requires me to stay out of rivers, streams, and saltwater.

Bass from Freeze's Pond, at Jay and Audrey Clugston's home, with Jack and Elle, Gainesville, Florida (June 2021).

Strangely, on our next-to-last fishing trip together, my GPS with all my "hotspots" ceased to function. It was an old model, and I couldn't transfer location numbers to a new model. It was difficult to give up boating, but rather than selling my 2000 Key West, Jay and I agreed he would take over ownership. A mechanic checked it out and found a major and costly problem with the 140-horsepower Johnson motor. Jay got a good deal on a boat and trailer—not so good with the outboard.

Audrey, Jack, and Elle, with the 2000 Key West Bay Reef boat on Lake Winnott, Florida (May 29, 2021).

Without my boat, now my fishing is limited to cane pole fishing for bass and bluegill in Jay's pond with his two children, Jack and Elle—but I am fishing. I still—and will always—read the weekly "Area Fishing Report" in the local newspaper.

Chapter 10

TRAVEL

ALASKA

In September 2011, I joined four Gainesville friends from Trinity United Methodist Church on a fishing trip to Kodiak Island, Alaska—where I had been offered employment about fifty years before. The trip was to include a day trolling for salmon, three days of bottom fishing, and an ATV trip to the Salmon River. It was late in the season; the weather turned very rough, and we were limited to about two days of bottom fishing where we caught many halibut (the largest about eighty pounds), Pacific cod, and lots of black rockfish (four to five pounds each). The inshore creeks were rising and became unsafe for an ATV trip. In lieu of that trip, our guide took us to two riverbanks to cast for salmon. The first was under a bridge, and results were unsuccessful with the lure our guide provided. I switched to a Little Cleo spoon that I had in my "pocket" tackle box. Almost immediately I caught two pink salmon and had a few other strikes. At the second site, where the Russian Creek joins the open sea, the banks were lined with fisherman. Some had "stringers" of nice silver salmon, but it appeared the biting had ceased for some time. All appeared to be casting a lure similar to that offered earlier by our guide. Using my Little Cleo, on my third cast I caught my first (and last) silver salmon; I also caught and released my first and only Dolly Varden. Unfortunately, none of my partners were successful. This does sound like a little

Fishing trip on Kodiak Island, Alaska (2011).

bragging, but, a key point is to always carry a few of your most reliable lures regardless of where you are fishing. It was a great trip, and we all came home with about one hundred pounds of frozen fillets of halibut, cod, and black rockfish. The processor added a few salmon fillets to each of our take home packages to help keep us happy, which was really not necessary because we all had a great experience!

After I retired, Marilyn and I traveled nearly every year. Our first adventure was on a Sky Princess cruise to Alaska in May 1998. Prior to our cruise, we spent a few days in Seattle, Washington, on our own. We then sailed from Vancouver via the Inside Passage and made numerous stops at interesting ports along the Alaska coast. We traveled on a motor coach to Anchorage. En route we stayed at a lodge, and, on a free day, I arranged a fishing trip on the Kenai River where I was introduced to "back trolling" for salmon. I had one great strike but didn't catch any—but the wildlife and scenery were worth the trip. Marilyn enjoyed a white-water rafting trip while I fished. From Anchorage we traveled on the Ultra

Dome train through Denali National Park and on to Fairbanks. This trip really whetted our appetite for travel.

IRELAND

Our next trip was on a motor coach tour through Ireland in 2002. Ireland was of special interest since we both have Irish ancestors. Marilyn's grandmother was Bridget Kearney, and the Belfast phone book is full of Clugstons. We extended our trip a few days and traveled on our own with a rental car—my first experience with driving on the "wrong" side of the road. Roundabouts were my biggest challenge.

NEW ZEALAND

In researching future trips, we discovered Overseas Adventure Travel (OAT)—a company that usually limited most of their trips to fifteen or fewer people. OAT also emphasized the physical requirements for their travelers; there was frequently hiking or walking required. In addition to the scenery and environment, OAT focused on the history and culture of the native people of the countries we visited, and most of the trips included a dinner visit with a local family in their home so that we could meet and get to know one another across cultures. It all added up to a fun and educational trip!

Our next ten trips were with OAT or their parent company, Grand Circle Travel. In 2005 we traveled through New Zealand for nearly three weeks where the habitat varied from rain forest to glaciers. Our guide, who was part native Maori, had a degree in art history. Because of him, we likely learned more about his country than most travelers. We even experienced a small earthquake on the South Island to round out our New

Zealand experiences. Near there, we had a fish and chips lunch at Smithy's Tavern in the small town of Haast. This bar is considered by some to be one of the closest bars to the South Pole.

THE AMAZON

We did not waste much time and in 2006 took an Amazon River cruise through the rain forests of Peru on a houseboat. On a few evenings and very early mornings, we traveled in a large jon boat into small coves (or we hiked on land, with rubber boots and a strong flashlight) to see the many animals that normally moved around at night. We also were able to photograph movement, such as it was, of the sloths in the trees overhead. The trip advertised fishing for piranha, and it was my only disappointment of the trip. We fished in a small cove with primitive cane poles (and they were *primitive!*) for about thirty minutes. Marilyn caught one piranha, and I caught a catfish unlike any I had seen before.

TANZANIA

Our trip of a lifetime was in 2008 when we went on a safari to the Serengeti of Tanzania. We traveled in three open-top Jeep-like vehicles so that we could stand on the seats for better photography. On one occasion a herd of elephants suddenly changed directions and surrounded our vehicles. We were advised by our guide to *not do anything* as they walked by, but we could have easily reached out to touch one.

The trip was advertised as a "luxury tented safari," and except for some nice lodges at the start and end of our trip, we did sleep in very nice tents that had a toilet and shower. Outside each tent was a large bucket of water on a pole, and then gravity would force the flow of water to the shower head. The attending support staff kept a large bonfire going, so if the shower water was too cold you would simply yell, "More hot water, please!" and they would replace the water in the shower bucket with heated water. It was a tough camping trip!

Every evening a lighted lantern was placed outside the tent entrance to keep unwanted animals away, and each tent was supplied with a whistle and a machete. We were told to blow the whistle only for a real emergency. One evening Marilyn woke me up—she had heard a large animal walking around the outside of our tent. The sound eventually disappeared, and we did not blow the whistle. We later learned that a lion had been prowling around our campground. The trip was for those with a sense of adventure, and I would do it again if I could!

MACHU PICCHU AND THE GALAPAGOS

In April 2009, Marilyn and I ventured to Machu Picchu and the Galapagos. This trip was eighteen days long and included tours of Lima and Cuzco, Peru. We did a lot of high-altitude hiking (to 11,000 feet), took a four-night cruise in a small ship around the Galapagos Islands, and spent a few days in a Galapagos hotel for land exploration. With the help of our guide, I did get to fish. My fishing guides were three generations of one family—a grandfather, his son, and his grandson—none of whom spoke English. We trolled a few hours for a species unknown to me, but I was fishing and happy! I did not catch any, but the scenery was fantastic! Marilyn and the rest of the group spent that time on a boat observing wildlife, and a few people snorkeled.

Fishing trip in the Galapagos Islands, Ecuador (2009).

COSTA RICA

In 2011, we stayed a little closer to home and visited Costa Rica. We traveled throughout the country in a minibus, from sea level to an altitude of 6,000 feet and saw amazing birds and other wildlife. We rode on horseback, went zip-lining, and survived some whitewater rafting. On a free afternoon, with the help of our guide, I arranged a tarpon fishing trip in a nearby river. The boat could accommodate three fishermen. Jerry, a traveling companion from Michigan, wished to go, but no one else from our tour was interested. While in a restaurant in a remote village, Jerry and I talked over the upcoming fishing trip. A man on a nearby barstool overheard us and expressed interest, so a country doctor from England joined our fishing party. We walked about a mile to the riverbank and met our guide. His boat and the fishing gear he provided were very well used. I fished with a spinning rod and an eight-inch mirrOlure with most of its mirror effect worn off. We cast along a number of shorelines and eddies. Near the end of our time, I finally had a strike when a huge tarpon took the lure. It made three jumps and on the third jump broke free. The fish nearly straightened two hooks on one of the treble hooks on the plug. Because I had caught thirty- to forty-pound tarpon in Florida, my companions were more excited than I was to see the biggest fish they had ever seen on a fishing line. I would guess, though, that this tarpon was eighty to one hundred pounds.

RIVERS OF EUROPE

We and three other couples from Gainesville joined a river cruise to see "The Great Rivers of Europe" in 2013. The vessel accommodated about 140 people. We started in Amsterdam and traveled on the Rhine River, the Main River, and Danube River through Germany and ended in Vienna, Austria. We passed through many locks along the way to change river systems and stopped many times to see medieval architecture, learn the culture of the people, and shop. Although we were on the water most of the time, I couldn't fish because of local regulations. I did see some men fishing along the banks with cane poles.

GREECE AND CROATIA

Marilyn and I traveled on a smaller vessel, with only forty passengers, from Athens, Greece, to the Dalmatia Coast in Croatia in 2015. En route we visited many small ports in Albania and Montenegro. In Croatia we had interesting land excursions in Dubrovnik, Korcula, and Split and then disembarked for good at Zagreb. Here a highlight of the trip was a hike within Plitvice Lakes National Park, which has sixteen turquoise lakes linked by a series of waterfalls and cascades. That day was Marilyn's eightieth birthday—a great way to celebrate!

ICELAND

We joined some Gainesville friends on a trip to Iceland in 2016. This trip was our last overseas adventure. The habitat was diverse—from the modern city of Reykjavik to farming communities and fishing villages. The scenery ranged from green valleys and craggy mountains to areas of hot springs and eerie lava fields. We saw the Gullfoss Waterfall, visited the "Blue Lagoon" (a geothermal pool), climbed a glacier, went whale-watching, and marveled at the diverse bird populations in such different environments. One memory, perhaps the "lowlight" of the trip, was tasting a traditional Icelandic dish—*hákarl* or "rotten shark"—made from Greenland shark, which is poisonous to humans. Early Icelandic settlers would bury the fish in dirt, where it would ferment. Then, they would cut the rotten, fermented meat into strips, dry it, and eat it. Today, fermentation can be accomplished without burying the shark, but the taste remains much the same—like ammonia. Marilyn and I each tried one bite; it was all we could take. Fortunately, they offered a strong alcoholic drink, a potato liquor called *brennivin*, to wash it down.

The whale-watching trip was supposed to include fishing for Atlantic cod, but the fishing was limited to a few rods that were passed back and forth between the people who wished to fish. I was unsuccessful with my turn. However, Bill Buhi, a member of our Gainesville group, caught a cod and was kind enough not to hold this success over me. We all enjoyed a lunch of very fresh cod after we were back on land. Overall, the seafood was great (especially the mussels), and every day was delightfully different. The air temperature was cool to cold, but not unpleasant.

It is difficult to describe these trips in a paragraph or two. Each day of each trip offered good learning experiences and adventure. The small number of passengers on most trips permitted us to interact with residents of each country to learn much about their history and culture. We usually enjoyed a meal hosted by the residents—even on the Amazon River where the food was served on banana leaves instead of plates. We left each trip having made many new friends of our fellow travelers— some of whom we correspond with today.

PROFESSIONAL TRAVEL

I've been fortunate over my career to attend many professional meetings throughout this country and around the world. Many times Marilyn was able to join me on these trips. When we lived in Athens, Georgia, it was common for neighbors to take care of our two children so Marilyn had a chance to travel with me, and, in turn, we would keep neighbors' children so that their spouses could travel. Grandparents were usually willing to help as well.

In 1996, I was on the steering committee for the Third International Symposium on Sturgeon, Piacenza, Italy, which was an excellent travel opportunity for Marilyn and me. I was fortunate to participate in similar symposia in France (1989) and Russia (1994). Marilyn was able to accompany me to France.

It's pretty evident that I have touched a lot of fish in my life, but I did other things, too—though much was related to fish, our waters, and our overall environment. I worked in Florida as a fisheries biologist for seven years at the beginning of my career and then worked elsewhere in the Southeast for about eighteen years before we returned to Florida to live in Gainesville. The population growth, natural habitat loss, and alterations that occurred over those eighteen years were dramatic. These changes stimulated me to become involved in local and state environmental issues. In the meantime, I kept up with old friends and colleagues from my earlier years of work in Florida.

ANCIENT ORDER OF FISHHEADS

Over the past four decades, the "Ancient Order of Fishheads" met almost annually. Original membership was made up of fisheries biologists and staff who were employed by the Florida Game and Freshwater Fish Commission in the late 1940s through the 1950s. I fit that category. The purpose was simply to have annual reunions at locations in the Southeast that were convenient for most to visit. During the ensuing years, some

First meeting of the "Ancient Order of Fishheads," Hickory Knob State Park, South Carolina (Jay and Leslie at bottom right) (1980).

changed jobs, most retired, and a few moved to other states, but most managed to return for the reunion if able. A few younger Game Commission employees joined the group as they retired.

Meetings were usually three days long at a site agreed upon by members. Host members or persons suggesting a specific site arranged accommodations with a meeting room for socializing. In the early years, we usually had a cookout that included fish or wild game. The host also recommended the best restaurants and arranged for visits to local attractions—although old and getting older, we were always ready to learn something about the areas we visited.

The first meeting was held at Hickory Knob State Park, South Carolina, in 1980. Marilyn, Jay, Leslie, and I attended. The group played volleyball, swam, hiked, rode horseback, told stories—and some played poker until late at night. About twenty-five members and their families attended the first

Final reunion of the Fishheads, Jekyll Island, Georgia (May 2019).

get-together. The next meeting was not until 1986 at Wakulla Springs, Florida, followed by trips to Helen, Georgia, in 1988 and Cedar Key, Florida, in 1990. Annual reunions began in 1992. Sites included Ormond Beach, Florida; Unicoi State Park, Georgia; Lake Point State Park, Alabama; Panama City, Florida; Red Top Mountain State Park, Georgia; Savannah, Georgia; George Bagby State Park, Georgia; and others. We visited some sites twice. The last official get-together was April 30–May 2, 2019, at Jekyll Island, Georgia. Age and health issues slowed many of us. Some children drove their parents to the meeting. We altered our physical activities and didn't stay up quite so late playing cards, and afternoon naps were added to the agenda. Over the years we heard the same stories about others and ourselves over and over again—but they remained funny, and we always had a great time. Thanks to email, many of us still keep in touch.

THE AMERICAN FISHERIES SOCIETY

I have been a member of the American Fisheries Society (AFS) since 1958. The AFS (founded in 1870) is the oldest professional society in the world representing fisheries scientists. During my more than sixty years as a member, I served as secretary-treasurer and president of the Society's Southern Division. I also was president of the AFS Introduced Fish Section from 1986 to 1987. I served on numerous AFS Committees such as the National Nominating Committee, Resolutions Committee, Water Quality Committee, and Executive Committee. In 1975 I was program chairman of the Society's National Meeting in Las Vegas, Nevada.

In 1975 I served on the steering committee for the First National Bass Symposium in Tulsa, Oklahoma. I also organized, served as program chairman, and compiled and edited the *Proceedings of the Fifth National Workshop on Environmental Impacts of Pumped Storage Operations, Clemson, South Carolina, 1979.* I also served on the Environmental Task Force, Southern States Energy Board, from 1979 to 1980.

SAVE OUR SUWANNEE

I joined Save Our Suwannee (SOS) in about 1996 and remained involved for about fifteen years. I was on the board of directors for much of that time. This all-volunteer organization was formed in 1993 and was successful in preventing a landfill from being developed about a mile from the Suwannee River. During the following years, SOS continued to monitor residential and agricultural development that threatened the pristine nature of the Suwannee River and alert the public of such activities by monthly meetings and newsletters. This nonprofit group disbanded in 2015.

SOS disposed of its treasury and donated $5,000 to Florida Defenders of the Environment, $5,000 to Florida Springs Institute, and about $6,000 to Fort White "Parknership," a collaboration between the school district and Ichetucknee Springs State Park. Fort White, Florida, is located four miles from the park, which serves as an outdoor classroom so students can develop an understanding of the land, air, and water that all living organisms depend on for life—all with the goal of instilling in the students their responsibility to protect our natural resources.

FLORIDA DEFENDERS OF THE ENVIRONMENT

The Florida Defenders of the Environment (FDE) is one of the oldest conservation organizations in Florida and is made up of a network of scientists, attorneys, economists, and other professionals and public citizens dedicated to protecting Florida's natural resources. One primary purpose of FDE is to coordinate the collection and dissemination of pertinent information on alterations of the environment and keep the public advised through meetings and newsletters. The group has been involved in numerous legal actions involving environmental issues.

FDE was founded in 1969 by Marjorie Harris Carr to help stop construction of the Cross Florida Barge Canal. An injunction was issued about sixteen months later to stop construction on the project. However, before construction was halted, a dam was built on the Ocklawaha River that created a 9,000-acre reservoir and covered about twenty natural springs. Unfortunately, the dam remains, and there has been an ongoing dispute between those who want to remove the dam and restore the river (such as FDE and other environmental groups) and some bass fishermen (many with strong political ties) who want to maintain the reservoir for fishing. I remember how the state and the Ocklawaha River looked in the early 1960s and believe restoring the Ocklawaha River by removing the dam is a great opportunity to reverse one of man's alterations of a natural environment. I hope we have a chance to see the river run free again!

I became a member of FDE in 1988. I have served as an adviser, trustee, treasurer, secretary, and an at-large member of the executive committee for many years. I have written short articles for their newsletter, *The Monitor*, over the years (see the appendix). I have considered myself as "support staff" to FDE whenever my experiences could contribute to understanding and resolving environmental issues.

Chapter 11

HUNTING

While I've focused on fishing, hunting has also played a role throughout my life. Hunting, especially in later life, met my need to be outdoors and sometimes supplanted my need to go fishing. I've spent many—too many to count—early mornings, late afternoons, and early evenings in the woods. Hunting can be controversial; many people frown on shooting wild animals for sport. But hunting is much more than shooting a rabbit, duck, or deer and then bragging about the harvest to other hunters. The opportunity to be on the edge of a salt marsh early in the morning and see hundreds of waterfowl soaring overhead is a scene to remember. If ducks are attracted to your decoys and you shoot one, it is hard to describe the joy of seeing your well-trained retriever bring the duck back to you. Because deer hunting requires patience, some hunters will sit in a tree stand all season and not see a deer legal to shoot, yet they return to the woods year after year. What many people might not understand is that while we wait, hunters see countless other wildlife moving through the trees—young deer, bobcats, wild hogs, raccoons, and many species of birds—all behaving naturally, unaware of being watched from above. Most hunters have a deep appreciation of the natural world and do their best to be respectful of it.

I grew up in a hunting family and learned to hunt at an early age. As a teenager, I remember a pre-dawn gathering at my grandfather's house—all my uncles, my grandfather, my father, and me—on the opening day of deer season. In Pennsylvania, at that time, deer season was only two weeks long.

One or two of our group was designated a "driver," and the others were assigned a "stand" somewhere on my grandfather's farm. Then at a given time and location, the "drivers" would walk through the woods toward those of us in a stand, hoping to flush a buck to the waiting hunters. My father was usually a driver, and I was usually in a stand. I was given my father's 303 Savage deer rifle to use—a big deal to me even though I never shot a deer on these hunts. I remember a large eight-point buck that my grandfather harvested. My father and uncles butchered it, and everyone got their share.

While in high school I hunted a lot on my grandfather's farm for squirrels, rabbits, and ruffed grouse. I shot at many flying grouse but hit very few. Jack Ifft, a high school friend, and I often hunted for rabbits on the open farmland around Stroudsburg. There were very few "No Trespassing" signs, and we could hunt almost anywhere we wished. One December, Jack and I were hunting rabbits in an unused portion of LaBar's Nursery (now a cemetery); we were walking near a small pond when a duck flew up. Without thought, I shot and it fell into the pond. The duck was well out of reach, but I wanted that duck—it was the first one I'd ever shot. Ignoring the snow on the ground and the fringe of ice clinging to the edge of the pond, I stripped down to my underwear and swam out to retrieve a beautiful male wood duck. It was only about twenty yards, but that was a mighty cold swim. I was very proud of this duck, and the following weekend we visited my mother's Aunt Meta and Uncle Frank in Girard-ville. I took the cleaned duck and gave it to them to eat.

I wasn't able to hunt during my first two years of college or the two years while in the army. However, after returning to

Penn State, I became interested again in deer hunting. I bought a 300 Savage, Model 99, rifle at the bookstore in downtown State College and hunted in an area known as the "barrens" not far from Penn State.

Later, after I graduated with my master of science, Marilyn and I moved to Fort Lauderdale where we acquired a beautiful Weimaraner puppy, Heidi, who soon accompanied me to work in the Everglades and nearly everywhere I ventured. A work friend was training a black Labrador retriever to retrieve ducks, and we joined him. Heidi learned quickly, and she made a great water retriever. In turn, I became an avid duck hunter just to watch her retrieve ducks. A move back to Leesburg provided a great opportunity to see her work. The lakes around Leesburg abound with waterfowl in season and unlike today, there were almost no alligators to worry about.

We bred Heidi once, and she had a litter of eight puppies. They all sold quickly, but one went to a fellow worker who was also a duck hunter. A few years later we hunted together, with mother and daughter retrievers, on the shores of Mosquito Lagoon at Cape Canaveral.

Our move to Galveston also provided some great duck hunting. A few laboratory members had a small hunting lease in a nearby salt marsh, and I willingly joined the group. We would leave Galveston at about 4 a.m. on the ferry, drive to our lease, and walk a levy to the spot where we had about fifty decoys hidden in the marsh. We deployed the decoys just as the sky was getting light and waited in our makeshift blind for incoming ducks. During our second year in Galveston (1965), Heidi retrieved forty-five ducks—plus one blue goose—on twelve hunting trips. She also retrieved ducks for others hunting with me, so she did retrieve lots of birds that year. We were usually

Successful duck hunt with Heidi, Galveston, Texas (1965).

back to work by 9:00 although I cannot guarantee the quality and quantity of work we produced on a hunting day. And I left this job to move to Georgia!

The move to Atlanta two years later changed my hunting opportunities greatly. Because co-workers and others I befriended were deer hunters (and without much duck habitat close by), I began to deer hunt again. When I had the opportunity to duck hunt again in Georgia or later in South Carolina, I hunted wood ducks in beaver ponds. The hunting was an early morning hunt, waiting for the ducks to fly into the pond to feed after roosting somewhere during the night.

Deer hunting is a waiting sport that requires much patience. It requires some scouting to find signs of deer activity, perhaps to find a "scrape" or "rub" that indicates a buck in the area. After finding a promising spot, I would place a tree stand nearby and after a few days return and hope.

When we lived in Georgia and South Carolina, most of my hunting was on public game management land. I had a camper top and built-in bed in my Ford F-100 pickup truck and would often camp near a hunting site on a weekend and be ready for early morning hunts. Florida also had many well-managed game management areas that I took advantage of. Because of their popularity, small size, and good hunting, some areas used a lottery system to control the number of hunters at one time. My favorite area was the Big Shoals Game Management Area. It is a unique habitat in Florida with steep slopes and hardwood trees near the banks of the Suwannee River. I shot a ten-point buck with my crossbow there in 2011. Unfortunately, it ran into a thick swamp, and my hunting companion, Buck Albert, and I couldn't find it. I returned two days later, and the odor helped me locate it. Despite the smell and abundant flies, I removed the antlers.

As most states, Florida, Georgia, and South Carolina offer special seasons to control harvest numbers but still provide ample opportunity for hunters to be in the woods. Usually an archery season is offered first, followed by a muzzle-loading rifle season. Modern rifle season follows. Florida permits hunters to use the two primitive methods in rifle season if they wish. I initially used a basic compound bow, but, because of arthritis in my left shoulder, I switched to a crossbow in bow season. I also hunted with a 54-caliber black powder rifle and my 300 Savage rifle that I purchased in the Penn State bookstore.

In addition to hunting public land in Florida, I joined a number of hunt clubs. The number of members depended on acreage available. The first two clubs I joined were purchased by land developers and lost to hunting and other recreation—the fate of much land in Florida!

In July 2004, using some of the money I received from selling the two lake lots in South Carolina, I purchased 120 acres near Rosewood, Florida, about an hour's drive from Gainesville. Half of the property was recently clear-cut pine trees, and the other half was a beautiful cypress swamp that had not been cut for many years. I purchased the land as a long-term investment for Jay and Leslie and as a managed recreational area for family and friends, as it is at the present time.

With professional help, the next year was devoted to chopping, burning, and bedding the slash pine site for future planting. In January 2006, we planted most of the area with about 44,000 slash pine seedlings. I also planted about 2,700 longleaf pines on a five-acre site, and about an acre was planted with 200 red cedar trees. The pine trees were planted farther apart than most tree farmers do who wish to maximize production and profit. I used a conservation plan that allows more sunlight to reach the forest floor and increase the plant growth that supports many other plant and animal species. Thanks to my nearby swamp, the area encourages deer, wild hogs, wild turkey, wood ducks, and all kinds of small mammals and bird life. A friend maintained some beehives on my land and shared the honey, but a black bear destroyed them. A neighboring property owner once called me to look at some footprints along a common road. Jay and I looked and took photos; later a wildlife biologist verified the tracks were made by a Florida panther. Both the bear and panther were probably just passing through—no one saw them. Our property does support many species of wildlife!

Over the years I spent many fall and winter days in the woods, and I've been lucky later in life to have memorable hunting trips. In September of 1994 and 1997 Jim Terrell and I participated in muzzle-loader elk hunts in Colorado. Jim had been a graduate student working on his master of science when I was assistant leader of the Georgia Cooperative Fishery Unit. We hunted deer together often at that time. Jim spent his career as a biologist in Colorado and lived in Loveland. Our elk hunts in 1994 and 1997 were in the Mt. Zirkel Wilderness area on the Continental Divide in Colorado. Kim Primmer, who also had studied at the University of Georgia when I did, joined the trip West mainly to fish in some of the high mountain lakes. I left Gainesville at an elevation of about 177 feet above sea level, drove to Calhoun, Georgia, at an elevation of about 660 feet, to meet Kim. We traveled together to Loveland, Colorado, at an elevation of about 5,000 feet. The three of us spent several days there, did some day hiking in the area to become acclimated with the altitude, and assembled gear and food we needed for about ten days on the mountain.

On the ascent day both years, we drove to a trailhead near the town of Walden, at about 8,000 feet, near the boundary of the Wilderness Area. We began hiking upward—I had about forty pounds on my back, and Jim had fifty-five pounds on his back—and we both carried our muzzle-loading rifles. Kim helped us in the first part of the climb but remained at a lower level to camp and fish.

The first year, Jim and I hiked upward of about 9,000 to 10,000 feet, near the tree line, but a little lower the second year to set up our campground. We had a three-man tent to sleep in and keep our clothing and rifles dry. We wore Gore-Tex jackets and pants and had a large tarp to protect us from wind and rain when outside the tent. The weather was known to change dramatically and without warning. One night, following a nice day, lightning began to flash in the sky around us. We stored our gear and headed into the tent and waited. The storm struck with a vengeance—the nearly continuous lightning lit up the inside of our tent like a strobe. We covered our heads with our sleeping bags to drown out the light and noise while the storm beat down on our tent. Because we were near a tree line, we had no place to hide and had to ride out the scary storm in the tent.

The 1994 elk hunt did not decrease the elk population in any way. I had one opportunity but goofed. Jim called a large bull elk to come down the trail where I was waiting. It was about twenty yards away; I was being especially patient to get a clear shot with no brush in the way. Then without warning, it spun and went on its way. I never saw such a big animal move so quickly. I learned this was a little different from white-tailed deer hunting!

The 1997 hunt, as the first, provided gorgeous scenery. However, the area seemed home to more elk, and Jim shot a "little" 4-by-4 bull elk not far from our campsite. After field dressing and partly butchering the animal, Jim left me a piece of tenderloin for cooking and headed down the mountain with his pack loaded with elk meat. I remained in our camp for two nights and experienced being utterly alone in the wilderness for the first time in my life. The occasional sound of wild animals was all I could hear; there was no traffic noise or sound of another human voice.

One morning, as I crawled out of my tent, I was greeted by a large mule deer looking down upon our camp from a hill above the tent. Its massive body was highlighted against the morning sky, and he eased down by our camp and disappeared into the woods. I remember looking around at the peaceful setting; it was too perfect to be real—almost like a Thomas Kincade painting. I won't ever forget it. As I did every morning, I walked to the stream to splash cold water on my face to wake up. I was in no

Elk-hunting in Mount Zirkel Wilderness Area, Colorado (September 1994).

hurry to leave, so I made a cup of coffee on the small Coleman stove and fried the elk tenderloin for breakfast. It was the first meat I had eaten for days. I trusted Jim was on his way back, so I leisurely walked down a nearby drainage (the path the snow-melt makes as it flows downhill). I wasn't hunting but carried my muzzle-loader since some of the wildlife would eat people if given the opportunity. Along this walk, I encountered a por-cupine; I hadn't seen many in all of my time in the woods, but it was enormous. Luckily, he went his way, and I went mine. Ground squirrels and chipmunks, curious and unafraid of me, were everywhere. I doubled back to the drainage where we camped, so I didn't go too far and get lost. It was a perfect day.

I've been fortunate to hunt in some beautiful areas, whether in Colorado or in the Southeast, but I won't brag about how many antlers are hanging in my garage. Marilyn doesn't appre-ciate animal parts hanging around the house, but in my office I have one set of antlers hanging on the wall. It is from a perfectly proportioned eight-point buck that weighed 148 pounds (field dressed). I shot it in 1978 on a South Carolina farm. I usually limited myself to one deer a season, which provided ample ven-ison to freeze and eat throughout the year. While Marilyn didn't want to see the deer I brought home, she was always willing to cook venison, and we have had many delicious meals from the deer.

There is another hunting trip I will always remember—but not because of my hunting success. My grandson, James Andres, had been in the woods a number of times with his father while living in Kansas. His family usually visited Florida during the brief time doe hunting was permitted. I took James to my hunt club shooting range to practice with a borrowed youth model 243 caliber rifle, and in 2015 I took him on his first deer hunt.

We were in a two-man tree stand, and a group of about six does approached. James remembered his instructions on patience well but waited too long. When they were about ten yards away, he moved his rifle to shoot—and they scattered. He also remembered that shooting at a running deer is usually unsuccessful and a waste of ammunition. Still, this was a great experience and fun for both of us.

We tried again in 2016. This time, a single doe came into view at about thirty yards. James aimed carefully and made a perfect heart shot, and the seventy-five-pound doe dropped in its tracks. James was just ten years old. He may or may not grow up to be a hunter, but he has learned some of the basic skills if he wishes to pursue it. And his grandfather will always be proud of him, regardless of what he does with his life. Now James is going on fifteen, has earned his second brown belt in Kenpo karate, and is three steps away from a black belt. He is an excellent student who will succeed at whatever he does.

My final hunt was at the age of eighty-five during archery season. On the first and only day I hunted, I shot a six-point buck with my crossbow on my timberland near Rosewood. I was hunting alone (something a man that age was told never to do). While driving home with the deer in the back of my Ford F-150, I found time to call some of my hunting companions and tell them of my success—I had to brag a little!

EPILOGUE

It has been quite a trip.

As a child, I played in small streams, catching minnows and crayfish and learned to identify the resident wildlife by their footprints. I had a father who took me blueberry picking in a cranberry bog where the earth and nearby trees moved up and down with every step. I got my feet wet, and it was great fun. I also learned the birds of the bog by their sounds from the surrounding trees. I was in the woods constantly, seeing and feeling nature all around me.

When I first moved to Florida sixty-two years ago, I was fascinated by the availability of wild places—but even then, they were being lost to the "progress" of the tourist industry and development spurred by the influx of new residents fleeing cold Northern winters. Consequently, too many people have not experienced true nature or wilderness—and they never will. Contented to remain in their air-conditioned houses, they fertilize their lawns, to the detriment of the waterways, and spray their backyards for mosquitoes and all other possible insects, killing important pollinators.

I hope we wake up to all we are losing. I hope my grandchildren, James, Jack, and Elle—and everyone's grandchildren—will be able to experience all of the wild places, unspoiled. I hope they will have their time at the top of the mountain. I have been there, and it is a great place to be.

AFTERWORD

TRIBUTE TO JIM CLUGSTON, GENTLEMAN ANGLER, SCIENTIST, FRIEND & COLLEAGUE

by Kenneth Sulak

The Reel Story is indeed the real life story of Jim Clugston, family man, outdoorsman, scientist, colleague, friend, and gentleman. His memoir captures the spirit of the "compleat angler" and outdoorsman that was at the very core of his being from an early age. His childhood fishing became a lifelong passion and morphed into his adult profession as a scientist devoted to the study and conservation of fishes. In Jim's lifetime, the old tease was that the professional society to which all fishery biologists really belonged was not the venerable American Fisheries Society, but the mythical "Hook and Bullet Club." Jim Clugston was indeed a lifelong member of that august fabled fellowship of anglers and hunters, whose members also happened to be fishery biologists—and whose fish stories grew grander with each reunion. For generations, angling and fisheries biology went hand in hand, a social tradition ensconced as well in small informal groups. Jim and his family were part of such a fishy fellowship, "The Ancient Order of Fishheads," from inception in 1980 to its last meeting four decades later. For Jim and fellow fishheads, there was a fundamental physical and spiritual connection between work and play, job, and family. He never went anywhere without his trusty take-down rod and companion box of favorite lures and an eagerness to cast a line out on the nearest body of water at any opportunity. Once, after a torturous all-day Florida Bay conservation meeting in Key Largo, I was ready to crash, but Jim was ready to fish. After a hasty meal, he dragged me to a nearby canal under the Keys Overseas Highway where we fished for snook until dawn.

Sometimes, we trolled for sea trout off Suwannee or Cedar Key. As his regular fishing buddies would attest, Jim was hard to outmatch in enthusiasm, fishing skill, and fish boated. He outfished me every trip; if I landed one keeper, he boated five. But, even when the fishing was sub-par for both of us, Jim had a good day on the water. His hunting buddies, even the much younger ones, told much the same tale. Heading into the woods from the vehicle, Jim was raring to go and hard to keep pace with when heading to his tree stand.

Until the advent of high-tech remote sensing and computer simulations, the standard boots-on-the-ground tools of the fishery biologist were small boats, nets, trawls, traps, waders, and angling gear—pretty much the same toys of the recreational angler. Getting hot or cold, wet, tired, muddy, sunburn, and pestered by bugs was part of the job and the whole outdoors experience. Sadly, that traditional tie between the personal and the professional has faded as remote sensing, sophisticated telemetry, and chairborne computer simulations have replaced old boots-on-the-ground and hands-on field methods. Jim was among perhaps the last generation of that ancient fishhead breed for whom plying the fisheries profession truly meant getting wet and dirty. He had a special reverence for the lure and the magic of nature. His epilogue here reflects a bit of sadness about the continuing loss of natural areas and the need to preserve the vanishing human connection with nature in its wild, unaltered state.

Jim Clugston was a lot more than just a fish biologist who loved to fish. He was a serious scientist who left a lasting legacy in developing knowledge critical to restoration of the imperiled Gulf Sturgeon. When Jim arrived in Gainesville, netting and tagging had already been ongoing in Florida, but in fits and starts, lacking well-defined conservation objectives. Jim built the new US Fish and Wildlife Service Laboratory, teamed up with Frank Parauka, and got serious about sturgeon science. Together, these two remarkable and consummate professionals took the reins of what became a four-decade program of Gulf Sturgeon population and conservation research in the Suwannee and Apalachicola rivers. That program soon turned into the template for parallel research in all seven Gulf Sturgeon rivers, Florida to Louisiana. Eventually, it achieved regional, national, and international impact. Jim's program spawned the first Gulf Sturgeon conservation research workshop, with eight scientists attending. Within a decade, the workshop morphed into an annual three-day conference with as many as eighty participants. Wider recognition came during Jim's lead, with continuing impact after his retirement, as Gainesville sturgeon scientists were invited to present papers at several International Symposia on Sturgeon, and to serve as founding board members of the North American Sturgeon and Paddlefish Society.

In the final year of his life, Jim knew his time was drawing near. He confided to me that he had one task to complete and he was determined to getting that done. One last big fish to land.

Jim wanted to leave a heartfelt legacy for his children and grand-children, an autobiography centered upon his love of fishing, hunting, the outdoors, and his family. With his typical spirit and drive, and that signature smile on his face to the end, Jim did indeed find the strength and wherewithal to reel in and preserve that last big fish.

APPENDIX

STRIPED BASS IN SILVER SPRINGS—THEN AND NOW

First published in The Monitor *33/1 (April 2016): 4–5.*

My career as a fisheries biologist began in 1959 when I was employed by the Florida Game and Freshwater Fish Commission (now Florida Fish and Wildlife Conservation Commission). Although I worked on assignments statewide, most of the next seven years were spent conducting research in the lakes of central Florida. I was introduced to Silver Springs at that time, and, fresh out of a northern university, I was amazed at the clarity of the Silver Springs and Silver River and the abundance and diversity of the fishes easily seen from the glass-bottomed tour boats. About 25 fish species were believed to be in the spring run. Those commonly seen were largemouth bass, bluegill, spotted sunfish, and other members of the sunfish family, channel catfish, striped mullet and the striped bass.

In September 1963, I assisted in a census of striped bass in Silver Springs and about 4.5 miles of the Silver River. My job was to drive the boat slowly downstream and tow two other biologists in SCUBA gear to count the striped bass seen to their left and right. About 400 were counted at that time.

I left Florida in 1965 and worked for the U.S. Department of the Interior in Texas, Georgia, and South Carolina. Except for an occasional meeting and one trip as a tourist, I saw little of Florida until I returned in 1983 to oversee construction and serve as Scientific Director of the Fish and Wildlife Service's laboratory in Gainesville.

During my absence of about 18 years, the face of central Florida had been greatly changed by Disney World, the Villages, and countless other developments. The Rodman Dam on the Ocklawaha River was completed in 1968. Over the last few decades, tourists riding the glass-bottomed boats at Silver Springs find a greatly reduced fish population—and no striped bass are seen. However, every spring since the completion of the dam, local newspapers have reported excellent striped bass fishing in the Ocklawaha River at the base of Rodman Dam. Undoubtedly Rodman Dam stops migration of striped bass and other species upstream in the Ocklawaha River and to the Silver River and its numerous constant-temperature springs. Removal of the dam will permit striped bass to reach the springs of the Silver River—the thermal refugia important for their survival.

DO BASS FISHERMEN REALLY NEED RODMAN RESERVOIR?

First published in The Monitor *36/2 (November 2019): 7.*

Florida is often touted as the "Fishing capital of the world." The Florida Fish and Wildlife Commission (FWC) points out that there are three million acres of lakes, ponds, and reservoirs available to fishermen in the state. Rodman Reservoir, on the Ocklawaha River, is about 9,000 acres at full pool. The FWC also reports that Rodman Reservoir is one of the top 10 most popular bass fishing waters in Florida. Many of the other top bass fishing areas are a short drive from Rodman Reservoir. Fishing is cyclic in most lakes and reservoirs, with good and bad years. At present, Rodman Reservoir is in the "good fishing" category.

Over the past few decades, there has been an ongoing dispute between environmentalists, who want to remove the dam and restore the river, and some bass fisherman, who want to maintain the reservoir for fishing. The environmentalists emphasize the importance of a free-flowing river for the benefit of all flora and fauna, many of which are listed by Florida as endangered, threatened, or of special concern. Without the dam, striped bass would be able to migrate to the constant temperature springs of the Silver River to survive summer heat, and manatees could visit the springs for winter survival. On the other hand, fisherman point out the reservoir's excellent bass fishing and economic benefit to the nearby communities.

Rodman Reservoir undoubtedly helps the economy of Putnam County; it attracts both casual fishermen for recreation and competitive fishermen for numerous bass fishing tournaments. A recent two-year study by the University of Florida examined both the public preference for and economic impact of restoring the river to its natural state versus maintaining the reservoir as it is now. UF researchers concluded that total expenditures and economic impacts of visitor spending for recreational activities in the existing natural portions of the river are about twice as high as they are for activities on the reservoir.

Do bass fisherman really need Rodman Reservoir? The fishing is good, but it is as good in many nearby lakes and rivers. This prompts another question—if the fishing is so good, why do tournament fisherman leave the Rodman Reservoir by way of the Buckman Lock to fish in the St. Johns River if they have the opportunity?

A two-year study in 2004 by James Livingston, then Ocklawaha River Restoration Project coordinator for Florida Defenders of the Environment, was to determine the location and sizes of winning catches in Putnam County fishing tournaments. His data is from 177 tournaments as reported in the *Palatka Daily News* from February 2001 and August 2004. One of his findings for tournaments starting in Rodman Reservoir was, if given the chance, tournament winners left the reservoir to fish in the St. Johns River. At that time, the river was considered the most consistent bass fishery and had the largest bass.

The exit from Rodman Reservoir to fish in the St. Johns River continues today. The annual Save Rodman Bass Fishing Tournament includes in its rules the Buckman Lock operating schedule so that fishermen can leave the reservoir to fish in the river and return to the starting point in the reservoir in time for the official weigh-in at Kenwood ramp. As reported in the *Palatka Daily News*, top winners in the April 6, 2019, Xtreme Fishing Tournament caught their fish in the St. Johns River. Karen Chadwick, operator of North Star Charters on the

Ocklawaha River, counted 20 tournament boats coming back through the lock after fishing in the St. Johns River during an April 20, 2019, tournament.

Fishermen are weird people. I know because many of my past and present fishing companions and I fit that category. An avid fisherman for the past 75 years, I have always found a place to fish wherever I lived or visited. Given the ready availability of good fishing waters in Central Florida, I believe Rodman Reservoir fishermen will do the same. Perhaps they will also enjoy fishing in the scenic environment of a restored river. There are also always ample tournaments in Palatka and other sites on the St. Johns River to meet that need.

Natural areas in Florida are constantly being lost because of the influx of new residents and the infrastructure required to accommodate them. Florida's population is now 21.6 million people and projected to reach nearly 26 million by 2030. New toll roads are planned that will open large areas of natural lands to more development. Even with our present population, Florida waters are suffering because of increased nutrients (primarily from lawn fertilization, outdated septic systems, and agriculture) that result in algae blooms and other health issues. Water withdrawal from our dwindling aquifer is of ongoing concern because of home, business, and agriculture needs.

I realize I am describing a bleak picture for the Florida environment. I remember how the State and the Ocklawaha River looked in the early 1960s. Restoring the Ocklawaha River by breaching the Rodman Reservoir dam is a rare opportunity to reverse one of man's alterations of a natural environment. Hopefully you and I will have the opportunity to see the river flowing free again.

ACKNOWLEDGMENTS

When Dad awoke from the surgery to implant his peritoneal dialysis catheter in July 2019, he said he had dreamed he wrote a book. I offhandedly replied, "Well, why don't you?"

I didn't know then that it would be the beginning of his two-year journey of writing, fact-checking, selecting pictures, calling friends to ask questions, and more writing—all long-hand and on legal pads—writing that age and arthritis made barely legible even to Dad, let alone to anyone else. For two years, we talked about "the book" during almost every phone call and in quite a few emails; he wrote the final piece, the epilogue, in late June 2021 after I arrived in Gainesville for the first time in eighteen months. All along the way, I had promised to get the book into print and to make it look as professional as I could. But I knew I'd need help from good friends.

First, I am grateful to Kenneth Sulak and Steve Robitaille, who both read the manuscript, answered questions, and offered feedback. These men, both friends and colleagues of Dad's, meant a great deal to him, and he was excited to have them contribute to the book. Thank you both for helping me see this through.

I am grateful to Leo Whitman, fellow Buchholz High School '88 alum, who set up voice-to-text on Dad's computer, taught him to use it, and, more importantly, made sure the book file was both autosaved and somewhere Dad could always find it. Because of Leo, Dad was able to read his manuscript pages into Word when his fingers no longer cooperated on a keyboard. Then, in the middle of the pandemic, after lightning took out the computer, Leo returned, rescued files off the old hard drive, and set up voice-to-text again on the new computer.

I am also grateful to Dave Jones, my longtime friend and Smyth & Helwys colleague, who not only converted the color images to black and white and made sure all the pictures look as they should but also guided me through the process of getting the book printed.

Finally, I am grateful to Victoria Frayne, whose beautiful cover design captures the feel of the book so perfectly. The day Dad got sick, Vickie came to Gainesville with Eden, kept me company, hung out at the house so James and Eden could visit while I was at the hospital, fed them—and then set up the book's page design for me that hectic week.

So in July 2021, I was able to finish the typeset and add the photographs while sitting with Dad in his room at North Florida Regional Medical Center. While he never got to see the printed book, he looked over every page on my laptop and seemed happy with it. And because of the help of generous friends, I was able to keep my promise. Thank you, thank you.

—Leslie Clugston Andres
August 2021

IN MEMORY OF
JAMES PAUL CLUGSTON
JUNE 28, 1933–JULY 14, 2021

Jim, Leslie, Marilyn, and Jay on the Key West Bay Reef boat,
Lake Santa Fe, Florida (June 16, 2021).

Made in the USA
Columbia, SC
03 September 2021